Luna and the Heart of the Forest

Luna and the Heart of the Forest

ADAM KARLIN

BREAKWATER BOOKS
P.O. BOX 2188, ST. JOHN'S, NL, CANADA, A1C 6E6
WWW.BREAKWATERBOOKS.COM

A CIP catalogue record for this book is available from Library and Archives Canada.

Cover Illustration: Brooklyn Mitchell, Gair Designs Inc.
ISBN 9781778530081 (softcover)
© 2024 Adam Karlin

ALL RIGHTS RESERVED. No part of this publication may be reproduced, stored in a retrieval system or transmitted, in any form or by any means, without the prior written consent of the publisher or a licence from The Canadian Copyright Licensing Agency (Access Copyright). For an Access Copyright licence, visit www.accesscopyright.ca or call toll free 1-800-893-5777.

We acknowledge the support of the Canada Council for the Arts.
We acknowledge the financial support of the Government of Canada through the Department of Heritage and the Government of Newfoundland and Labrador through the Department of Tourism, Culture, Arts and Recreation for our publishing activities.

PRINTED AND BOUND IN CANADA.

 Canada Council for the Arts / Conseil des Art du Canada

Canadä

 Newfoundland Labrador

Breakwater Books is committed to choosing papers and materials for our books that help to protect our environment. To this end, this book is printed on a recycled paper and other sources that are certified by the Forest Stewardship Council®.

For Rachel, Sanda, Isaac, Dad, and Mom

Acknowledgements

I am humbled that the publishers at Breakwater Books trusted me, an outsider, to write a story about their home. To that end, I am indebted to the people of Newfoundland who welcomed me into their homes, pubs, restaurants, boats, and businesses. I can say, without hyperbole, that I received a warm welcome wherever I went on that island. I cannot adequately express my gratitude in the face of this hospitality and generosity. This book is a poor expression of the affection I have for Newfoundland, but from the heart, I can say that it was written from a place of respect and reverence. Thank you in particular to Laura Rock Gaughan, Marnie Parsons, the entire staff at Breakwater, and my editors, Susan Hughes and Geoff Pevlin.

I wrote the first draft of this novel while on a ten-day writing retreat at the Virgina Center for the Creative Arts. Early readers there included Ginny Mohler and Erica Vital-Lazare, and I wouldn't have been at VCCA without the support of faculty from the University of New Orleans Creative Writing Workshops, particularly M.O. Walsh, Richard Goodman, and Barb Johnson, all teachers and authors whose attention and care have immeasurably improved my craft. I also want to recognize my fellow UNO MFAers, and the general New Orleans literary community, who have been a source of unflagging support and friendly feedback, including my brother, Christopher Romaguera, as well as Elizabeth Brina, Erinn Langille, Ross Nervig, Blake Carpenter, Caro Fautsch, Dan Sutter, Tad Bartlett, Bryan Washington, Maurice Ruffin, and anyone else who has tipped back a few at the Parkview.

Other sources of writerly support include We Need Diverse Books, who awarded an early draft of this novel a Walter Dean Myers Grant, and the Breadloaf Community, especially Christina Berke, Sarah Cadorette, Mary Terrier, Eleni Linas, Kirtan Nautiyal, Alex Morris, Neysa King, Tim Bradley, Isaac Zisman, Phil Saint Denis Sanchez, and Marcela Fuentes—thank you, thank you, thank you.

Friends from Maryland, New Orleans, and beyond have facilitated my writing since very early days: Adrian Van Young, Mike Robertshaw, Jonah Evans, Rob Lalka, Mark Matthews, Dan Matthews, Christopher Frates,

Stefanie Covey, Jay Dreyer, Raina Zelinski, Angela Watkins, and the faculty, staff, and students at NOCCA, to name a few.

Finally, I reserve my greatest thanks to the people this book is dedicated to: my parents, Wayne and Ohnmar Karlin, my wife, Rachel Houge, and Sanda and Isaac. You last three, in particular, deserve nothing but the best, but have instead gotten a dad and husband who has spent weekends and weekdays and too many nights writing and revising. I'm sorry, and I'm so, so grateful. I could not have done this without you. You three are the reason I do anything and everything.

Disclaimer

While *Luna & the Heart of the Forest* is set in Newfoundland, I have invented all of the locations within this book. Dove Cove is an amalgamation of several different outports from across the island. Angie O'Riordan's abandoned home is similarly cobbled together from notes and impressions I took after walking through the ruins of multiple resettled communities. There is only one working paper mill in Newfoundland, located near Corner Brook. The mill I have described in this book is only partially based on the Corner Brook mill; it is also inspired by similar buildings in the US.

Like Luna, I have always been a lover of myth, legends, fairy tales, and folklore. The creatures, magic, and monsters presented in this book are inspired by Newfoundland's landscape and cultural heritage, but they are also products of my imagination, and mix elements of stories I have encountered around the world. With all of that said, it was the island of Newfoundland that brought these things to life, that called them out of the recesses of my imagination, and it is to that island that this book is indebted.

I cannot overstate how rich and varied Newfoundland folklore is. For those readers who want to learn more about the topic, I highly recommend a visit to the Newfoundland & Labrador Heritage website (heritage.nf.ca).

And yet my heart wanders away,
My soul roams with the sea, the whales'
Road, wandering to the widest corners
Of the world, returning ravenous with desire,
Flying solitary, screaming, exciting me
To the open ocean, breaking oaths
On the curve of a wave.

—*The Seafarer*, author unknown

1

Luna's father taught her how to speak like a Viking after she asked about the ghosts.

It was a reasonable question. A fog wrapped the island, thick and grey. It followed Luna and her dad as they drove past dark pine forests and ocean-kissed cliffs in their rented car. Luna thought the fog was mysterious, and possibly dangerous, so of course she wanted to explore it. But Luna was Luna, and that meant questions came first.

"Big Bear?" Luna said from the backseat of the car. She used the nickname she invented for her dad when she was four. She was eleven now, and it felt weird, almost baby-ish, to call him that in front of other people. But between the two of them, he was still Big Bear.

"What's up, kid?" he said.

"Could there be ghosts in the fog?" she asked.

Her dad grunted. He grunted a lot and wrestled and ate every meal like it was his last and gave hugs that lit a fire in Luna's heart. He also slept like a log and snored like the chainsaw that cut the log, which were all ways he'd earned his nickname.

"If there were ghosts around, they'd definitely be hiding in all this cloud murk," he said, his brown eyes catching her green ones in the rear-view mirror before switching back to the road.

"What's a *cloud murk*?" Luna asked.

"The fog. But I used a kenning to say it." Big Bear glanced at Luna in the rear-view mirror again.

Luna raised her eyebrows, which was her way of saying, *A what?*

"That's a way the Vikings would describe things," he said. "Like little poems, where a few words were tied together to describe something, but sideways. So fire was the *bane of wood*. Blood was *battle sweat*. The sea was a *whale road*."

Luna thought this sounded clever, and she wasn't the type to miss out on a chance to be clever. So, she invented a few kennings of her own. The car was a *metal horse*. The overcast sky was a *dark blanket*.

She looked at the shore. Back home she might call the beach a *sand belt*, but there was no sand here, just boulders, stacked like grey marbles against the ocean. The waves pounded the rocks as if they wanted to drag them into the ocean, and Luna thought of Vikings in battle as she thought of a kenning for the rocky coast: *stone shields*.

"Why are you talking like a Viking, Bear?" Luna asked.

"Because the Vikings were here, in Newfoundland." Her dad stressed the last syllable of the name so it rhymed with 'understand.' "They crossed the ocean to get here, way before that jerk Columbus. They were great explorers. Like you."

"Like *me*?"

"I mean, leave out the sacking and pillaging, then yeah, sure," Big Bear said.

"So my kenning would be *Viking Girl*."

Her dad made a 'who farted' face, and Luna laughed.

"No way," he said. "I just told you, the Vikings were pretty brutal. Plus, it's hard to make a kenning for someone because people are more than one thing. But I guess, if I had to, I'd give you *cat curious*. Because you always poke your head everywhere. Even in places that I tell you are dangerous." He turned his head and made an exaggerated angry face. "Except cats get nine lives, and you only have one."

She knew her father's words were more serious than his playful tone implied, but Luna was in a good mood and didn't want to get into an argument. So she smiled, leaned over, and touched Big Bear's arm. He took one hand off the wheel to squeeze her back, then quickly put it back.

On the road, a squeeze was often the best kind of conversation, and Luna and Big Bear were always on the road. He was a journalist, working for magazines, TV programs, and radio shows. He went to places, met people, took pictures, shot footage, wrote articles—in short, he found interesting stories and told them to the world. It was exciting work. Most of the time. Sure, when people asked Luna if her dad's job was an endless adventure, she thought of the days when he didn't change out of his pajamas and stared at a laptop until he remembered they needed dinner and ordered takeout. But other memories of their adventures glowed: swimming across rivers in deep green gullies. Riding horses over a desert painted blood red by the sunset. Sipping soda in a roadside diner where a friendly waitress showed off pictures of her grandchildren.

Luna's life was very different from other eleven-year-olds and also, in a lot of ways, very much like other eleven-year-olds. When she wasn't off on trips with Big Bear, she went to school and raised her hand in class (probably more than the other kids, if she thought about it) and, more or less, turned in her homework on time. Her teachers loved her work habits and were, at best, amused and, at worst, afraid of her constant questions.

She had sleepovers with friends where they decorated make-believe homes on Kindles and iPads. Luna was almost always the first to tire of screens and divert the night into a discussion on what kind of superpower everyone would want (she always veered between shapeshifting and weather control), before inevitably proposing everyone sneak out for a midnight wander around the neighbourhood in search of foxes or racoons or abandoned houses—the sort of creatures she could imagine shifting into, the sort of places where she could imagine using her powers against, say, a witch who stewed children into potions they drank to prolong their lives.

The journeys with her father were a disruption to this normal kid schedule, but Luna wouldn't have traded her life for any other adventure—because her life *was* an adventure. She got to see the world and learn from it. Being clever wasn't just about *using* her brain, it was *filling* it with as much as she could. Sometimes Luna thought of herself as a sponge, soaking up all the Earth had to offer. One of her clearest memories of her mom, besides the long, autumn-leaf red hair she had passed on to her daughter, was the time she pulled Luna out of kindergarten for a week-long camping trip. When Luna protested, because they were learning about reading clocks that week, her mom kneeled and whispered, "Don't let school get in the way of your education."

"But don't I need to learn to read clocks?" little Luna asked.

Her mom kept her voice soft as an early-evening summer breeze.

"You can learn all sorts of stuff in school," she said.

"But there are other things—the way light hits leaves, or the smell of the ocean, or the circles a bird makes when it flies—that you can only learn out there in the big wide world. And you, my moon, are going to shine your light *everywhere*."

"Why'd you name me for the moon, then?" Luna asked. "Doesn't the sun shine brighter?"

A crooked smile cracked her mom's face. "Yeah, but the moon has more fun. It gets to do stuff in the dark."

Back in the car, the memory made Luna grin. Mom had been gone for six years, but Luna was often in her own head, and in that active space her mother came to life, the gaps in her memory filled by the stories of her relatives. The list of contributing family included Luna's dad, of course, and also her pwa pwa (dad's mom), who lived in Singapore, which was very far away, and gaga (mom's mom), who was in New Orleans, which was easier to visit.

Gaga always snuck a chocolate into Luna's pocket whenever she came to visit. Luna and her grandmother would chat for hours, gaga telling stories about her daughter, each tale a daub of paint that, over time, swirled together into a portrait: of a soldier, a risk-taker, an adventurer, and finally, for five happy years—before the accident that took her away—Luna's mother.

"The thing to remember about your mum was that she was, first and foremost, a rolling stone. Just like your pop," gaga once said when Luna was eight and had stopped feeling too shy to ask questions about her mom.

"What's a rolling stone?" Luna asked.

"Your mom liked to move. That's why she joined the army—so she could see the world," said gaga.

"And she joined the Medical Corps and became a doctor so she could help the world," Big Bear said.

"And she married you because you liked adventures same as she did," gaga added.

Big Bear chuckled while he stroked his black beard with copper-coloured hands. "She was more the wanderer than I ever was," he murmured. "At least, she was always more willing to conveniently ignore a No Trespassing sign or a fence if it came between her and where she wanted to go."

"Our people don't mess around," gaga said, chuckling, as she touched Big Bear's arm.

But Luna agreed with her dad. Sure, Big Bear liked to travel. He even made a job out of it. But her mom had been—and this was gaga's word, not Luna's, so it was OK to use it—a *hellraiser*. She didn't just have adventures; she broke rules to go on them, like the time she snuck off her base so she could climb a 1000-foot hill, watch the sunrise, and be back in her barracks before anyone noticed she was gone. For the last year or so, Luna had started feeling like not all rules made the most sense, and stories of her mom breaking the ones that got in the way gave her heart a flutter—one that was a little nervous, but mostly exciting.

Big Bear? He *liked* rules—making them, following

them, and especially making sure they were followed. He made sure Luna filled out math and English workbooks every day, decided when she could have snacks and when she could have screen time, and enforced her bedtimes with a drill sergeant's precision. For a guy who liked to explore the world, Luna thought her dad sure liked to build fences. Around her, at least.

Luna liked to swim because feeling water on her skin was a way of getting wrapped in an element she didn't usually live in, but whenever she wanted to take a dip at the beach or in a river, Big Bear went in first to check currents and water temperature. Luna liked to go for walks because it was the simplest, easiest adventure someone could have, but even *that* was a process weighed with rules and conditions; her dad, for example, was always careful to cover her in long pants, sunscreen, and bug spray ("Can't be too careful with ticks").

But worst of all, Big Bear had begun to insist, effectively, that Luna not leave his side. On her last birthday they had gone to a state park anchored by a three-mile loop trail. Luna asked her dad if they could split up: he would hike the loop in one direction, she would walk the other, and they would meet somewhere in the middle and decide which direction to finish the trail in.

"But that means someone has to backtrack," her dad said.

"I knooow," Luna answered. "But I've never hiked on

my own using a trail map, and I really want to try," she said (all the while fairly confident Big Bear would agree to backtrack if she asked him to).

He finally relented, and Luna spent a grand couple of hours picking her way along clifftops that overlooked toothy gorges and resting her head on neon-bright patches of soft moss. True, she'd ventured a little off trail when something caught her eyes, but the route was well-marked with bright blue blazes and the park was popular besides; she was always able to hear other passing hikers and find her way back to the main path. Which she had just found when her dad came rushing down the trail from the other direction, sweaty and red-faced, and saw her stumbling in from the woods.

"*Luna*," he huffed. "You went *off trail*?!"

"Mom called it boonie stomping," she said, a little sheepishly, a little defiantly.

"Kid!" Her father did not seem to care what mom called it. "I didn't think we'd meet exactly in the middle, but I just walked three quarters of this loop on my own. I started asking everyone I passed if they had seen you."

"There was cool stuff in the woods," Luna said, a little less sheepishly, a little more defiantly.

"Next time we hike, you stick by me," Big Bear snapped. And that was that. These days, if the two of them went somewhere together, he could be counted on to freak out if she left his side. That hurt, because when her dad told her about things like kennings, or took her to places like Newfoundland, she felt as if the world was unfolding for her, like life was a painting, and new ideas and places were fresh colours she wanted to add to the canvas. But thanks to all his worrying, it was like her father had opened the door to an art museum, given her a peek—then shut it and hid the key.

Still, looking out the window of the car at the fog in the branches—*like a shadow sea*, Luna thought, coaxing the kenning out of her busy brain—she had to admit, her dad's job *did* get her around. And, as much as Luna had seen in her eleven years, which was more of the world than people five times her age, few adventures excited her like this one. A few months before, after getting home from school, her dad motioned her over to the globe in his office. He traced his finger along the US East Coast, past New York City and Boston, past Maine, past New Brunswick and Nova Scotia, landmasses like bony teeth chewing on the bright blue North Atlantic, until he settled on an island. An island at the edge of Canada, and the world.

"That will be home for most of the summer," Big Bear said.

Luna looked at the name—Newfoundland—and hopped onto her laptop. The more she found online, the more the little wings in her heart went from flutter to flap.

Soon she was neck-deep in pictures of haunting beauty: salty shores sliced by knife-edge rocks; candy-coloured homes; black bogs frosted with ice in midsummer, all plunked in an ocean surrounded by whales and icebergs. The fairy tale landscape called to Luna, who thought a mythology book on a cold night was pretty much perfection.

Exploring had always filled Luna's heart up till now. But just *seeing* wasn't enough anymore. She wanted to be knee-deep in the bog while snow danced across the sky; she wanted to feel the spray of the grey ocean tickle her face. Here was a picture of a cave: rocky, hungry jaws swallowing the saltwater on a bleak coast. Luna saw the bare trace of a path leading from high cliffs into that wet, black gullet. She had been consuming myths since she started reading, and the photos she found online spun into a dream: of picking her way amidst the rocks into the cave, where she would stumble into one of her favourite stories, the one of Loki stealing the necklace of Freya, the goddess of beauty who travelled in a chariot pulled by cats.

She'd see the trickster disguised as a seal sitting on a rock, the jewels of Freya glinting beneath his wet fur. The seal would tell her funny stories and tease her, because his wit was sharp as his soul, then beg her to hide him from the vengeance of the gods, who always had to control and tell everyone where to be and what to do.

Luna would help Loki, the clever seal. Because that was what you did on *quests*—you went with the magic of the moment—and this island, this cold fist of rock and pine, looked like a place where quests were as common as winter snow and salty storms. But also, she would help the trickster because they both loved adventure, and they both knew: *real* adventures could not happen with the gods—or your father—breathing down your neck. Her mom told her to learn from the wide world, but right now, at the edge of all the beauty and wonder that world promised, there was still a fence. If Luna ever found the narrow path that led to the sea cave, she knew she'd find Big Bear there, standing guard.

From when Luna and her dad landed in Newfoundland, she decided the island was more beautiful than what the internet had promised. Even from the airplane, it beckoned. There was the deep, dark ocean crashing into the cliffs. Here were spiky grasses and shrubs clinging to rocks that made Luna think of sleeping trolls. Patches of snow still salted the land, even though it was late May, and back home, everyone was in shorts and sandals. The view from the sky made Luna want to pack her sandals into the bottom of her closet, lace up good walking shoes, and not worry about going home.

They got off the plane and picked up their rental car. A few moments later they were driving through the capital, St. John's, to the top of a high hill, where they watched the wind blow over an ocean freckled with ice.

This is a cold land, Luna thought, and then she whispered it out loud. Her father nodded, and said, "Almost, my moon. It's a Newfoundland."

Luna pointed down the hill. Two birds, dark as night, raced each other. They flew low and fast, and looked like they were about to smash into the rocks, but then they veered away at the last moment.

"*Ravens from the sea,*" said Big Bear. A thin, cold rain was falling, and it made water bead in his hair and beard. "Maybe a sign from Odin. Remember Odin?"

"King of the Viking gods," said Luna, thinking, briefly, of a grinning seal in a sea cave.

Big Bear nodded. "And a trickster, and a magician. And part of Odin's magic was sending out ravens, *huginn* and *muninn*, 'thought' and 'memory'—"

"—to be his eyes and ears. I remember, Bear," Luna said. She squeezed her dad's hand, and he pressed back.

He sighed, and his breath made fog. "The Vikings loved ravens. They called their raiders 'sea ravens.' And another name for warriors was 'feeder of ravens.' Because ravens ate the dead after a battle. Whenever ravens showed up, it meant danger wasn't far away."

Luna thought her heart would jump from that cliff and flap its own wings just then. Because Big Bear mentioned *danger*. Quests didn't happen when your parents were holding your hand, but they did happen in places where danger wasn't far away.

Big Bear suddenly gasped as the two birds surfed air

currents up the cliff to the outcrop where he and Luna stood. They landed, hopped, and made a noise: *quork*. Luna looked into their eyes: shiny night mirrors, and their feathers, so black they held rainbows, like when she closed her eyes and colours burst in the dark.

Dark light. Midnight wings, thought Luna. Her mind had become a *kenning crafter*.

The rain kissed her cheeks and whispered in her ears. She watched the ravens hop, hop, then spread their wings, like a shadow falling on the island.

Quork. Quork.

2

Luna and her dad ended up spending a lot of their time in Newfoundland gasping at the view from various cliffs. So she wasn't surprised when, a few days after they saw the sea ravens, Big Bear turned into another cliffside parking lot. He often made little detours when he worked. Because he had to take pictures on assignment, he was always on the lookout for a good photograph. But he also did it because he was the kind of person who would stop whatever he was doing to look at something interesting.

Luna understood this habit of her dad's because she had inherited it—there was a reason she had taken so long on the loop trail on her birthday. Although the impulse went back much further. She remembered, when she was younger, Big Bear sighing on their walks because she would stop every few steps to examine this extraordinary weed or that tanning lizard.

Once, Luna recalled, Big Bear had said, in a huffy, let's-get-going voice, "Luna, do you have to smell *every* rose?"

She looked at him curiously and said, "Daddy, don't you do the same thing?"

And for a moment he stood there, before he grinned like a dope, said, "Fair enough," and waited for her to start walking.

That was then. In the now, Big Bear had gotten slower, while Luna had grown fast and fiery. These days, whenever she went somewhere it was like two voices were arguing inside her; one still wanted to smell every flower on the path, and one wanted to get to where she was going yesterday. She had managed to become both impatient and exhaustive when it came to exploring, and she was proud of it.

So she welcomed this latest highway cliffside stop. There were woods all around the horseshoe-shaped parking lot, except for the eastern edge, which faced the ocean. The fog had settled in the trees, and Luna wanted to see it up close, without the barrier of a passenger window.

Luna was fascinated by Newfoundland fog. The first time she noticed it had been when they started driving along the island's crinkled coast. Ropy strands of wet cotton weaved into the trees, a cloud of off-white and grey.

Big Bear had called it cloud murk. She liked that but added her own kenning: *milk thick*. It looked so wet she thought just staring at it made her clothes damp. The mist drew her eyes like moths to a flame; it was all the more mysterious because peering too long into the milk thick made it even more opaque.

Anything could be in there, she thought, as Big Bear looked for a place to park. She briefly glanced at the ocean, then looked back into the fog and the dim outlines of the trees beyond, her mind stretching to make room for *anything*: maybe something wonderful, maybe something terrible. Either way, it was largely concealed by the milk thick curtain. Luna wasn't sure she wanted to know what was behind that curtain, but she also wanted, more than anything, to know what was behind that curtain.

Suddenly, she saw something—a something that made her suck in her breath, then exhale forcefully and fog up the window, which made the view outside even fuzzier. She rubbed the window, wiping away her own mist to see the mist that lay beyond.

It was thin and long and curved and . . . *crooked*? She realized, against all sense and logic, that it was a finger in the fog. And it was beckoning to her.

At least, Luna thought it was a finger. Whatever it was, it was dark and—she was pretty sure—*sharp*, and it danced at the edge of her eyesight. One moment it was a shadow stroking the fog. The next, it became a man perched on animal legs. Then, a spider, scuttling over a branch. Finally, a whisper flitting in between the branches.

She thought, *On quests, you go with the magic of the moment*. This was a moment, and there was the magic, and she wanted to follow it. Then Luna blinked and there was just fog, far as the eye could see, and that wasn't very far.

Yet she was sure: she *had* seen something. And that something had *danced*, although Luna wasn't sure if it was a happy jig, or the way a snake sways for a rabbit.

While she was so focused on whatever was in the fog, Big Bear had finished parking.

"Let's go," he said, his voice calling Luna out of her head.

They got out of the car. The fog was now completely—and oddly—contained to the forest, but Big Bear led her towards the cliff and the scenic view, all green grass and buttery wildflowers at the top and wave-spattered rocks at the bottom, an ocean to the ends of the Earth, the surface wrinkled by wind and waves. Luna and her father had seen many things together, but this sort of view made her knees go a little weak at how lovely the world could be and briefly pushed away the memory of fog fingers and the desire to chase them.

Luna sucked in a great gulp of sea air. She *liked* Newfoundland. Once, in an old book, she had seen a picture of a cottage in front of rolling hills. It was a springtime picture and spoke of sunny days and garden parties. It was pretty, and pleasant, and filled Luna with vague disinterest.

This island wasn't that. It was beautiful, but in a fierce, wintery way. It was a place for wind and waves, not fields and flowers.

The land and water, the rock and salt and seafoam and ice, made Luna feel bigger on the inside. It especially grew the part of her that other kids did not understand (particularly the kids who liked pictures of springtime cottages), the part of her that sat comfortably by itself and remembered her mom and preferred solitude to being around other people. It felt strange for sadness and solitude to feel big and filling, but it felt real too, achy and sweet all at once.

She leaned on her dad's arm.

"It's *cold*," she said.

"It's May. You know how mom grew up in New Orleans? It's colder here than it is there in the middle of winter. A month ago, a lot of this water was ice." He went back to the car and stuffed a hat over Luna's head. "Keep yourself warm, kid."

Luna swatted his hands away. She preferred her hair flowing free, or 'wild child' as her mom used to say. "*Look*, Bear," she said. "There's still ice there." She pointed at enormous blue-white icebergs bobbing on the water—pieces of winter that had gotten lost at sea.

"We're somewhere different," Big Bear said.

But Luna wasn't listening. She had turned away from the ocean to stare back into the woods, the ones that edged the parking lot. She told herself she had never seen trees like this before, but then she thought of some scary movies and realized she had. Yet the more she looked, the more she thought the trees were more *old* than creepy. It was a certain kind of old, though; not tired or faded, but solemn, and imposing. And *alive*. She peered at the trees for a long time, their whippy branches, their whispering leaves, and saw—

—*the something*.

There it is again, she thought, the fog finger flashing across her memory. *A finger of . . . a person?* For a moment, she swore she saw the outline of whoever the appendage was attached to. *But they're too small. And fast. And the legs . . . don't fit.*

I've gotta find it.

Big Bear was obsessing over getting the right angle to take some photos. As he peered into his camera, Luna walked away from him and into the trees. Emerald moss lumped over a forest floor where ferns fanned out between the trees, themselves thin and crusted with lichen. She had gone a few steps from the roadside, but a world away. By the ocean it was cold, but big and wide and *open*. There was nothing to fence the wind in, so it blew strong because it went where it wanted. But here, inside the forest, everything was *close*. There was a breeze, but it had to pick its way through the trees, and there were a lot of trees.

Luna walked deeper into the woods, just for a moment. It was like walking down the stairs of a scary cellar; she knew the light at the top of the stairs would grow fainter the further down she went, but she couldn't resist the urge to keep going and see just how dim the light became.

She dared the world to change more, then turned around. When she did, she saw the woods had taken her dare. Big Bear, the car, the cliffs, the dim glow of the sea, all the signs of the place she had just been in, were gone. Instead, she saw branches and roots. The pine needles glistened with early morning frost, even though it was mid-afternoon. The moss gave off a growing, green sort of smell, musty and damp, the scent of dirt after a long rain.

There were woods behind her, and woods in front of her. No; that wasn't true. There were just woods, because backwards and forwards had become meaningless. Directions were replaced by trees, trees, mist, and more trees. Luna's insides bubbled, simmering dismay and excitement together.

The novelty of not knowing where she was felt a little exciting. At first, at least. She wasn't sure which way was what, so she just walked, to an unknown where. But the more she walked, the tighter the plants pulled in. The weak grey sunlight shrank into pin pricks in the tree canopy before it disappeared behind the branches.

When Luna had stepped out of the car a few moments ago, it had been cold. But the chill in the forest was stronger. It seeped into her bones. And as she walked further into the woods, it dug deeper. She rubbed her hands on her elbows and stamped her feet until she felt the ice in the air melt a little.

Then she saw *it* again, running through the woods. *There you are.*

She glued her eyes to the shadow. It was a little thing, barely taller than her five feet. Its shoulders were thin, and its arms were long, especially compared to its body; they looked like arms for scooping animals out of mud, or maybe their own shells. But the legs were strangest. They bent at an impossible angle, *or they would if they belonged to a human*, Luna thought, *but not to a horse, or a goat, or a deer.* But this thing moved upright.

Or at least, it looked like it did, until a cloud enveloped it, and it faded into the fog.

The same fog that was coiling around Luna's feet.

Luna froze.

Mist slithered up her like a milky snake; first, around her ankles, then up to her waist, chest, and almost, her face. Once it got there, she'd be sightless, and all alone, in the cold, old woods.

A thought made her stomach twist. She had read about fish that lived in the deep sea, swimming in a forever midnight. They bobbled lights at the end of their noses to lure smaller fish towards hungry mouths filled with needle teeth so long and sharp their jaws couldn't close. As the fog and the forest closed in, Luna wondered if, by following the shape into the woods, she was playing the part of a curious fish, swimming towards a pale light.

In the distance, she heard laughter—a cruel, cold giggle—on the wind. No; the laughter *was* the wind.

Then that thin, airy sound was swept away by a thunder crack. Only one thing could bellow with that sort of force. The thunder was Big Bear yelling, "Luna!" at the top of his lungs, a shout followed by twigs crunching and branches snapping.

If her dad called her name like that on any other day, she would have known she was in trouble. Now her heart leapt into her throat. Her dad was coming to help her, living up to his nickname, bellowing and swinging his arms, sweeping aside branches and leaves and more—the very *tightness* of the woods, the thick of the fog, unravelled under her father's huge hands. Luna wasn't the sort of girl who wanted to get rescued, but her heart suddenly ached for her dad to make everything all right.

Then: there he was. Big Bear scooped Luna into his arms and crushed her to his chest. She hugged back, tight, relieved, and suddenly, exhausted, even as—"Oof"—she felt the air squeeze out of her lungs.

"*Luna*," Big Bear said, breathing hard. "Oh my God, I was worried." He put her down, grabbed her by the forearm, and started pulling her away. The same hands that clubbed fog and branches gripped Luna so tight pain arced through her arm.

"Ow!"

"C'mon. I almost got lost following you in here. We need to go. *Now*."

It was the *Now*, that impatient, angry, careless command, that made Luna briefly forget how happy she had been to see him.

"I'm *fine*," she said, and it didn't matter if it was a lie; what mattered was not being led around like a dog on a leash. With a tug that seemed to surprise her dad (and even her) with its strength, she wrenched her arm free of his hands.

Big Bear reached out again; again, Luna pulled away.

They looked at each other in silence, the tension thick as the fog that had lured Luna into the woods. Then her dad shook his head and gestured at her to keep moving.

Luna's face fell. She hated being ordered around, but she was also well aware that moments ago she had been surrounded by a fog that wanted to devour her. So she moved in the direction Big Bear was heading—quickly, but moving *now* because she wanted to, not because he told her to.

She wasn't sure how they reached the edge of the forest so quickly, but soon she could hear the sea, glimpse the pale sky, then flashes of sun reflecting off the car, and finally, they were out of the woods.

Luna stared at her dad. He was breathing hard, and sweat glistened on his forehead. Panic lingered in his eyes. Now, under the clear sky, outside of those claustrophobic woods, her brain felt cleaner. It was easier to admit: Big Bear *had* just saved her . . . from *something*.

Her wrists were still sore from where he grabbed her, but Luna tried to swallow her frustration.

"Hey," she said. "I don't know what happened. How did you find me?"

He frowned. "I'm not sure. I saw you, and then you walked past some of the trees, and you vanished. I couldn't even hear you, much less see you. For a minute I thought you left the forest, came back out, and walked to the cliff edge and . . . " his voice grew as brittle as a dry leaf, " . . . and fell, except I couldn't see anything but the beach when I looked over the edge. Then the fog around the woods got *thick*, and I wondered if you were in the trees." A shadow passed over his face. "Why the hell did you walk off like that without saying anything?"

She winced at his curse. She was trying to keep things calm. But he only used words like that in front of her when he was about to lose his temper.

"I . . . saw something. It was interesting. You pulled the car over to look at something, I saw something and went into the woods. Same thing."

"No, it decidedly is not. I didn't leave you behind when I pulled the car over."

"You didn't *ask* if I wanted to pull over," she said, defiance frosting her words. "You told me to always be curious. I was being curious." This was true, and besides, quoting her dad to himself usually got her back on his good side.

But not this time. "I also told you to always be careful. You conveniently left that part out. You can't just vanish like that, Luna. Not without telling me."

Her dad's voice was hard, and sharp; *I could cut myself on it,* Luna thought, followed, by *Don't get mad. Don't get mad. Don't lose it.*

Then she got mad, and lost it.

"*Mom* would've gone in," she said.

A storm passed over her father's face, dark as the clouds now massing over the nearby ocean. He paused. When he spoke again, his voice was anger spiced with sadness.

"Mom and I were a team. She would've wanted you to respect my rules, because she loved you and would've known I'm trying to keep you safe. Also: you're wrong. Sorry, but you are. Whatever gaga tells you, mom didn't break rules just for the sake of it. Sometimes, she got in trouble. But mainly, she *helped* people in trouble. She broke rules for a reason."

Luna crossed her arms. "Any time I try to do anything on my own it breaks your rules."

Big Bear looked like he was about to say something back, but then the fight left him, like air hissing out of a balloon. He looked away, leaned against the car, and cursed under his breath. Light rain had been falling; now it thickened into fat, chilly splashes. Her dad's head was bowed, his shoulders were slumped. Luna knew that posture—it was the same one he had when he looked at pictures of her mom on his phone.

Luna had seen something in the woods. It had drawn her towards it, and frightened her, but she didn't know what it was. She saw something in her dad right now: sad and solitary, big as a cold mountain, the feelings he had planted in her when he yelled at her. Now both of them were filled with the sort of sad that gets passed back and forth, growing with each hand-off. She knew that feeling, but it was scarier than the woods, because she didn't know how to deal with it.

Luna's curiosity pushed her to explore the world; the books and myths she read stitched a desire for adventure. But another part of her wanted to be alone—not always, not even often, but sometimes, sure as stone—and there was no alone like being on a journey, because then she could balance solitude *and* the part of her that wanted to see things.

Sometimes, when she was alone in nature, Luna would have conversations with her mom. Sometimes, she spoke with the plants and animals all around her. It was like finding company in a place without people. But when she wanted *actual* people again, she knew she always had her dad. Big Bear would be there, the other half of their pair. Which was why *this* particular after-a-fight solitude was scarier than whatever led Luna into the woods. They couldn't find the words to bridge their hearts, and the gap that was left felt vast as the ocean.

Luna wanted to say something, felt as drawn to speak and fill the silence as she had felt to enter the woods. But she couldn't shape what was in her heart into words.

Instead, she got back in the car, and after a minute, Big Bear followed her. Then they drove away.

3

A few hours later, as darkness slowly puddled across the sky, Big Bear asked Luna if she was all right. She knew this question really meant, "Were *they* all right?", were things OK as far as dad and daughter were concerned. It was the usual question her dad followed a fight with, and in the past she would answer, "I'm OK, Bear," with a smile, and mean it.

"I'm OK, Bear," she said with a smile, just like before, except she wasn't.

He held her gaze for a moment. She felt like her dad didn't understand her. And yet, when he looked in the rear-view mirror and she saw the sad in his eyes, she knew he did.

...

Big Bear had a few towns to stop at for interviews, where they stayed at guesthouses (filled with antiques and art made by the neighbours) or hotels (filled with carpets that smelled like office buildings). They ate burgers and pizza at restaurants where the waitresses complimented Luna's hair. Sometimes it was hard to understand them; the way the people of the island spoke was light and rugged at once, with a melody like birdsong balanced by a flinty core as hard as the rocks that jutted out of the beaches and pine forests.

Between interviews and towns, Luna and Big Bear took hikes. Every time they came to the top of a hill or cliff, they found new takes on a familiar view: grey, rugged beauty, stretching forever. They remarked on this to each other. But they didn't talk about how Luna always kept close to her dad. Once, on a quiet day on a quiet corner of the island, she saw the fog bleed over the spine of the small peninsula they were hiking on. Luna kept herself from peering into the fog for as long as she could muster the will, which was about five minutes, and sure enough, when she looked there were patterns in the murk, dark shapes playing in the milk mist. They looked like fingers. Or fishhooks.

She remembered what had happened before, but also: *she remembered what had happened before. If I follow the fog now,* she thought, *I'll know its tricks and traps.* And she took a step in the direction of the cloud murk.

Then Big Bear sighed: heavy and deep and disappointed. And in that moment, with the feelings of their last fight still fresh, like a scrape that hasn't fully healed, the weight of her father's disapproval kept her from going towards the fog. Instead, Luna took a step back, in the opposite direction of the murk, towards her dad, and stuck by his side.

They kept driving around. They talked about food and hotels and how lovely the land was, and not their argument, the memory of which had become like a stone in Luna's shoe—a little hard nugget of irritation she was aware of but did not speak of—until they had new things to talk about, like the house Big Bear had rented.

It was owned by a fisherman who lived on a peninsula that pinched the water like a crab claw. Luna and her dad drove through woods and over hills to get there, until the evening darkened into a deep ocean blue. The road curved and twisted before it led them into a small town, a spackle of brightly painted homes hugging a half-moon bay built on sea cliffs scrubbed clean by the ocean. A faded sign told them 'Welcome to Dove Cove.' The whole place looked like it had been plucked from a storm. The homes were rain-wet, wave-splashed, and rickety, and the yards were piled with wire cages—"lobster and crab traps," said Big Bear.

He went on about everything he had learned about fishing gear (apparently, a lot) from the interviews he had done with locals. Big Bear had a habit of learning about things, then lecturing at length on the topic to the closest person who would listen. Which was usually Luna, who was used to this behaviour and figured it was part of why her dad had the job he had.

Still, this evening, she suspected that while Big Bear *was* genuinely into lobster pots, he was also talking about what was outside to keep the two of them from thinking about what they were still feeling on the inside.

The car slowed down on the village's narrow streets, and Luna rolled down the window. The air was fat with saltwater, and the wind whistled like an angry ghost. It was wind on a mission, and that mission, as far as she could tell, was nipping noses, blowing hats off heads, and tossing around brightly coloured net floats.

They drove deeper into Dove Cove, around a grey harbour filled with boats, bent and bygone with age. Luna saw few people outdoors, just a few scattered souls huddling in jackets that made them look like shapeless shadows, quickly crossing the streets as if to avoid each other and the lashing wind.

Finally, Big Bear pulled up to a house painted pale green, the colour of a sea much warmer than the nearby waters. A gloomy night had settled in, and the place looked empty and abandoned. A spaghetti tangle of ropes rotted on the lawn.

"This is the address," Big Bear said. "That's weird. We're sharing the house with the guy who owns it, but it doesn't look like anyone is home."

He walked up to the door and pushed. It swung open.

Before he could motion to Luna, she unbuckled herself. The rain drizzled a hundred cold kisses on her face, but she ignored it and walked with her head held high, ignoring Big Bear's sharp intake of breath as she pushed past him and into the house.

It was very dark inside, but it was warm. Plates were arranged on the windowsills, alongside old paintings half glimpsed through the shadows: boats sailing through storms. Fish gasping on docks. A portrait of an old man with a hawk nose and eyes that followed a person around the room. Luna could see dust in the air. She breathed through her nose and thought the house smelled sharp, like the wood it was built from still wanted to be trees. That was it, Luna thought. The house smelled old, but also *alive*.

Narrow stairs led to a second story. The darkness around the landing looked like a yawning, hungry maw. Luna knew it was a bad idea to climb those steps.

She turned and said, "I'm going upstairs."

"Luna, stop!" Big Bear said, but she was already walking. Each step made a creak like a ghost caught between the floorboards.

Halfway up the gasping staircase, the second-floor shadows weaved themselves into a shape: tall and wiry. The outline of a person emerged, built like the coils of rope in the yard. Luna screamed. It was both a scared scream and a scream that tried to scare the shadow. The sound of it soaked into the walls and floorboards. When the scream stopped, it was replaced with stillness.

Then the shadow at the top of the stairs said, in a rough, but calm, voice, "Hullo. I'm Gordon. You must be the Americans who are staying with me. Welcome to my home. Sorry, I was asleep."

Luna, breathing hard on this windy night in a dusty home full of shadows and paintings of dead fish, tried to calm herself. "Hi. You just surprised me, is all," she said.

They stood there, staring at each other, Gordon at the top of the stairs, her in the middle. The quiet went thick again. Too thick for Luna's comfort, so she pierced it with a question.

"Why does your home smell weird?" She hadn't meant for the question to sound rude, but the scare Gordon gave her had scrambled her manners.

Gordon looked her up and down. Then his eyes flashed, and he laughed. It was the sort of laugh that asked for company, and Luna decided to give it some, because it asked so nicely.

"That 'funny smell' would be the wood stove," said Gordon. He definitely had the Newfoundland way of speaking; his words stretched high, then low, like a song had lost its way on the tongue. "The stove is filled with balsam," Gordon went on. "Like what you use for Christmas trees. This island is packed to the great gills with balsam fir trees. That's the smell."

An island of Christmas trees sounded all right. It certainly smelled good. Luna felt bad for saying the smell was 'weird.' *It's sharp, actually,* she thought, *and spicy.* Now, with Gordon at the top of the stairs, and Big Bear chuckling (he had yelped a little himself when Luna screamed), the house didn't feel so empty. With people and laughter, the house changed from funny paintings and creaks and old stairs into a cozy, warm cottage.

Although still: a little strange.

Warm was good, because outside was all bitter bite. Gordon helped Luna and Big Bear bring their bags inside, before his lips curled into a playful smile under his moustache.

"Want to see where I burn those Christmas trees?" he asked.

Luna understood, deep in her soul, that the answer to this question was very clearly "Of course," but she also knew her dad probably wanted to crash after the long drive. But Big Bear gave Luna a knowing look and said to Gordon, "I am sure that would be very appreciated by at least one of us." He winked at his daughter, and she beamed back, and suddenly their fight, while not forgotten, certainly felt forgiven.

The fisherman took them to the basement where he showed them the wood stove, a bulging belly of iron glowing soft and red with logs. It was interesting, but Luna spent more time looking around the basement. Pots clinked, and empty sacks hung on hooks. They pulsed in the hot air that periodically escaped the stove, drafts that Luna named *dragon's breath*. Thin shadows crept in the corners. They reminded Luna of a creature dancing in the fog.

Gordon looked at her, looking at the dark. "House feels a little creepy, huh?" he said.

"I like creepy," Luna said. This was true: she liked Halloween and dressing up, haunted hayrides and all that. But the creepy in Gordon's house went deeper. It was a little like the fog in the forest: unsettling but, somehow, attractive. If there were ghosts here, they wouldn't be silly decorations sold at a grocery store in October. The ghosts in this house—*or anywhere on this island,* Luna thought—wouldn't mess around.

Gordon nodded. "You like creepy? Lord bless you. You're in the right place. Because this island's got monsters on the mind."

Luna grinned up at him, and he raised an eyebrow. "That sounds fun," she said.

Gordon shook his head. "You're an odd one, aren't you?" he asked, although Luna could tell he meant 'odd' in a good way.

And besides, she reasoned, it was true: she was tall, powerfully built, fire-haired, a lover of myths and quests and books and cliffs and deep woods and ghosts. Gordon laughed when Luna enthusiastically nodded.

The fisherman showed Luna and her father to their room: small, with squashy beds; plump pillows; thick, soft duvets; and a few shelves packed with books. One small window let in a square of the cold night. Luna peeked into the gloom and saw streetlights. Through the wet glass they looked like fuzzy oranges. A pair of enormous black birds pecked the ground, glistening in the rain.

...

Over the next few days Luna spent most of her time following Gordon and exploring Dove Cove. A new place and person were a good excuse to exercise her exploring muscles, and, unlike her dad, Gordon didn't freak out when Luna did Luna things, like poke around a junk yard looking for pieces of scrap metal (almost gashing her arm open on a sheet of rusted tin) or climb hands and knees up the crumbled stone wall that ran along the side of the yard (coming perilously close to falling into a patch of bull thistle).

There was a lot to see. The homes were all painted a different vibrant colour, as if a rainbow had broken on the rocks, and fires burned in all of them, little roses in the frost. The fires must have kindled the souls of the people who made them. After watching the people huddle against the cold on their drive in, Luna thought anyone who lived here would be as chilly as the weather, but it was the opposite. The locals radiated warmth in proportion to the cold, as if to maintain the balance in all things. They smiled big, laughed loud, hugged a lot, served *very good* hot chocolate, and often told Luna how clever she was. How they envied her auburn curls, or how her green eyes matched her olive skin, still pale enough to glow pink when the winds blew in off the Atlantic.

"You know," Big Bear said to Gordon one morning, over breakfast, "I don't tend to like it when other writers call a place 'friendly.' People are nice all over the world. But the people here really are . . . "

"They're *super* nice," Luna said, as she scooped eggs off her plate.

Gordon seemed pleased by this observation. "Nice of you to say so. Well, we know how to treat guests. Especially when they bring a kid around."

"What do kids have to do with it?" Luna asked.

Gordon looked out his window for a moment before answering. "For a lot of us . . . our kids and their kids have moved away. That's tough on a town. Makes it lack laughter. It's a sort of sickness. When you get to be my age, you want a young face and a willing mind to share your wisdom with. God knows I long for my daughter, and she's almost as old as your dad."

Big Bear nodded. Luna could tell he wanted to ask more questions about Gordon's kid, but she could also see he was holding his tongue out of respect for the fisherman's feelings. Instead, her dad said, "It does seem like a common theme here. People love the island, but not the economy. Shoot, which reminds me: I need to type up some notes." He got up to leave the table, while Gordon broke out some homemade molasses buns for Luna. They were dark and sweet, but not the cloying sweet of grocery store breakfast cereal. This was deep sweet, with a lick of warming spice. As she bit into it, Luna grinned. Her main goal in Newfoundland was finding adventure, but eating more of Gordon's molasses buns ran a close second.

"How about some tea to go with that? I've got Irish Breakfast or Earl Grey," Gordon asked.

Luna quickly shook her head, which prompted a bemused, barking laugh from her host.

"My grandson won't touch it either, the rare times he visits," Gordon said. "You don't know what you're missing! Nothing fights the cold better than a good mug up. I'll put in lots of cream and sugar, OK?"

When she made up her mind, Luna didn't like to change it, and she especially didn't like to admit she had changed it. So although she thought his offer actually sounded pretty good, Luna tried not to let her face betray this, and said, "No, thank you."

Gordon chuckled. "Fair enough," he grunted. "I raised a little girl myself. I know when not to press it. Fine; if I can't give you tea, how about a story? It's a hell of a tale."

Luna nodded enthusiastically, even as she blushed. Gordon had said a grown-up word—not in frustration, or anger, but because he was comfortable around her—and that made her feel both embarrassed and a little grown-up herself. "Make it a scary one and throw in another bun," she said.

Gordon grinned, tossed Luna the bun, then sat back in his chair, sipping his tea. After a few slow pulls on the mug, he began to talk, low and slow. Like all good storytellers, he knew how to take his time.

"So, one day, when I was a boy just a little younger than yourself, I stayed out too late. I'd been playing in the woods, and when you're out in the trees in these parts, especially near night . . . well, it can be a bit much. All I'm saying is: sometimes you see . . . Things."

The way he said 'Things' very much indicated the word needed to be capitalized. Luna thought of shadows in the branches, of fingers tempting her into woods cloaked in milk thick cloud murk.

"So, I saw . . . I dunno. A Thing. Way past the vegetable patches that people kept at the edge of town, near the headlands where the wind always blows a gale. I saw something, man or beast I cannot say now and couldn't have said then, but I will say it seemed to blend the two together."

"What did you do?" Luna asked.

"Like a fool, I followed it. Right into the woods. Further and further *into* the woods. It'd be there and then not, like when you have a dream and wake up and the memory of it is at the edge of your head, but you can't hold on to it any more than a splash of milk in your fingers. Well, this little Thing keeps on a-moving and I kept on a-following, until I knew I was pretty well and truly lost." Gordon sighed. "And then . . . it was the strangest thing. By that point, I wanted to get out of there. I did. But I also *still* wanted to find the Thing. Come hell or high water."

"So did you find it?" Luna asked as she played the events of a few days ago over in her mind. The strange forest; the urge to follow, while suspecting she was walking into danger; wanting to escape, while wanting to know what she was *escaping from*. It was like listening to a song she knew all the words to.

"As I said earlier, I'm a fool. So, no, I did not find the Thing, whatever it was, but I made a hell of an effort!" Gordon said, chuckling. "But that's when I hear the cry. *Hyip. Hyip. Yip hip pip pip pip pip pip.* I look up and it's an osprey. A water hawk. I used to see one when I rode my bicycle after school, every day, gliding above while I cycled the coast path below. And I got to wondering if that was the same bird a-circling me in the woods. It felt like it was.

"This may sound strange, Luna, but it felt like it was warning me. So, I think to myself: what do I trust more? This bird who watches me ride home from school every day? Or this strange Thing in the trees? That's the thing about birds: they see everything. And the good ones watch out for those they care about. *Hyip. Hyip. Hip pip pip.*"

Gordon had started his story in a light mood, with a smile cracking his face, and a happy fire dancing behind his eyes. Luna could see that fire was gone now, and so was the smile. Now he looked haunted, as if telling the story had brought him back into the forest.

"Well, bird or no, I had already pushed into the woods, and even if I wanted to turn back . . . the trees were gnarled and thick. And it wasn't just that the trunks were thick; *everything* about them, the way they grew, the way they looked. You couldn't get your eyes around them. If I looked up, I didn't see sky: just leaves and branches, like fingers pressing me into the dirt. Even the air passing between the leaves made me think of my grandfather's stories about fighting at the Somme during the Great War. There was poison gas there, floating down the trenches, and it choked the life out of a man."

"So how did you get out? Did the osprey help?" Luna asked.

"It did, but not before it got *dark*. A dark that didn't just cover your eyes, but your *ears*, because it muffled everything. But here's the thing: even then, the sound of the bird was louder than the darkness that surrounded me, if you catch my meaning. I kept my ears open for its call, and I kept following that sound wherever it led. After— I dunno how long, maybe a few minutes, maybe a coupla months, there weren't no time in that forest—I found myself back at the border of the woods, and then I could hear not just the osprey, but the waves. I was by the sea. I took a great big gulp of the cold ocean air, and I tell you: nothing ever tasted so fine."

Luna nodded. She felt she had lived this story not long ago. It made her feel closer to Gordon, which was nice, but she was also a little jealous, because he had escaped the weird woods without anyone else's help.

"I'm glad you followed the osprey. But did you ever figure out what you saw in the forest?"

Gordon shrugged his shoulders. "God only knows. There are many Things in the trees and by the seas. Boo-men and Little People, fetches and fairies and the Crust Man. And Billy Goat Legs."

Luna wanted to know about all these ... Things. She'd never heard of most of them, or if she had, she thought they were friendly. Weren't fairies kind? Not by Gordon's tone, at least. But one creature sounded familiar, and disturbing, and awoke a strange curiosity in her.

"What's Billy like?" Luna asked, remembering the shape in the fog, with legs that didn't fit.

"Well, I haven't met him, mind, but I've heard stories. Plenty of them. And he's a mean one," Gordon said. "Meaner still because he comes at you nice-like. Invites you to be his friend. Makes you feel cozy. That's the trouble. Once you sit down with Billy, he makes sure you never gets up again."

"What do you mean?" Luna asked.

Gordon made a chomping sound. Then he said, "He's very greedy. And he's clever and stronger than you can imagine. But there's a way to beat him. It's by your brains, not your brawn." He tapped his head, then emptied his mug down to the dregs.

"Anyways," Gordon said as he washed up, "there's another monster a little ways from here. If you're near it, it can catch you anytime you step outside. Drive by and it even creeps into your car windows. It's a hell of a lot scarier than Billy."

Luna sat at the edge of her seat. "What is it?!"

Gordon laughed. "The smell of the paper mill. The overwhelming scent of absolute, unadulterated—" and he used another word, even more grown-up than before. "Sorry miss, after my kid moved away with my grandson, my sailor talk got worse. Anyways, you'll meet that monster tomorrow, Luna. May not smell good, but that mill and the logging that feeds it brought a lot of good jobs here. Your dad wants to talk to some people out there and I know a bunch of guys who work the mill, so I went ahead and arranged for him to head out there tomorrow to interview some folks. Are you going along with him?"

"Why wouldn't I?" Luna asked. She always liked to experience new things.

Still, the next day she learned firsthand why the paper mill wasn't exactly the top tourism attraction in Newfoundland. Her and Big Bear set out after breakfast. Sitting in the backseat of the rental car, Luna knew they were near the mill before she saw it, because she smelled it. And as Gordon promised, it *stank*, a smell that landed somewhere between rotten eggs and rusted metal.

"I guess that's the mill?" she said, her voice muffled by her hands, which covered her nose and mouth.

"That's it," said Big Bear. They had driven away from Dove Cove until they came to a place where brick buildings belched fog into the air. This was decidedly not magic mist rolling in off the ocean. It was a factory fart. Gordon had sort of prepared her for the smell, but not for the sheer amount of smoke, or the pipes that poked out of the land like insect legs. They had driven down a hill to come here, and from a higher altitude Luna had seen fallen trees stacked in piles like so many discarded toothpicks. She imagined the forests where those trees had once grown and dreamt of a poison patchwork of brown, black, and grey wasteland. She loved nature, found joy watching light bend through a leaf. The only thing that bent the light here was the cotton thick smoke.

"It's disgusting," she said.

"It smells bad," said Big Bear.

"No, not just the smell," said Luna. "It's all terrible. The stupid, smoky building. The dead trees it makes."

For a moment, she caught her dad's eye in the rearview mirror. They'd had plenty of conversations since their fight, but she had just disagreed with him, openly and honestly, and this was the first time since that argument that she had felt comfortable doing that.

Big Bear and Luna liked to argue, or as he liked to put it, 'debate.' Her dad believed discussing an idea was the best way to understand it; he thought an energetic argument was as educational as exploring a new place or reading a book. He had raised Luna to have opinions and be unafraid of saying them. He told her this was to keep her brain sharp, although she suspected he also just wanted someone to speak with on long trips.

A lot of her friends thought arguing was stressful. They knew Luna could be a force of nature when she felt strongly about something (which was a lot of the time). But Luna loved a good disagreement. It felt nice to have one that wasn't so personal with her dad again. But even if the warmth of Gordon's house had softened things between her and Big Bear, she could still feel traces of the weight of their fight by the woods. It made her feel a little less sure of herself, like she was holding something delicate that could shatter with the smallest nudge.

Her dad had paused the conversation as he moved into a line of traffic that was slowly snaking past the brick buildings. Finally, he spoke, his voice careful and measured—which was normal for him, but Luna wondered if he, too, was worried about picking at an old scab.

"It's not pretty," said Big Bear. "But kid, every local I talk with agrees: this island is beautiful, but it isn't doing so great when it comes to jobs. A mill has those. People have to earn a living to, y'know, live here. Right? The guy I'm gonna interview today is six generations deep on this island. He told me his job at the mill was the only reason he was raising a seventh generation here."

"Why don't they have work?" Luna asked.

"Well, a lot of people used to fish, or worked to support the people who fished, but then the fish everyone caught got very scarce. So, folks had to stop fishing, which meant they stopped working, which meant they had to either leave the province, or find another place to work. And this mill happens to be that, and there's not a lot of work around otherwise."

This all made sense, but all Luna could think of was how hard she had fallen for the beauty of the island, how sad those stacked trees looked. And how she wanted her father, just then, to speak to her heart and not to her head.

She shrugged.

Their car was stopped, waiting for a construction crew working on the road up ahead. In the time they had been on the island they had run into a lot of construction crews—the workers had to pack all their work into late spring and summer because the other months were too snowy.

She watched a man emerge from one of the brick buildings, whistling and grinning. He had a full, friendly face. Maybe, Luna thought, he would pick his children up from school later in the day.

"Do you think that guy who just came out of the building works there?" she asked.

"I'd imagine so," Big Bear said.

"So he cuts down trees?"

"I doubt that," her dad said. "They don't cut the trees here. That happens somewhere else. The trees that get turned into paper here are trucked in from elsewhere. I mean, I'm definitely skipping some steps, but long story short, I don't think that guy is out in the woods yelling 'timber.'"

"OK, he doesn't chop down the trees, but the mill he works at is *why* they chop down the trees. Do you think he's from here?" Luna asked.

"I'd imagine that too."

She frowned. "Then he's hurting his own island. Harming the most amazing environment I've ever seen. What's the point of living in a beautiful place if you make it ugly?"

Her dad shook his head. "Honey, I'd rather be in the woods than a clearcut, but c'mon. We aren't from here.

Should we tell people who are, who have been here for generations, how to live their lives? Are you really gonna tell him to quit his job because it's pretty here? If he leaves that job, he can't afford to live here, so he moves away. You know what happens when people lose their homes? It doesn't make a place beautiful; it makes it abandoned. A lot of people have already left this island because they can't find work. This is a place we're visiting. It's *home* for the people you're criticizing."

"But . . . " Luna paused. "Remember what you and mom always said? 'Home can be anywhere. Home is what you make it.'"

She didn't see Big Bear frown because he was in the front seat facing away from her, but she felt it.

"For us. I'm not telling that to someone else," he said, his voice a little disappointed.

"Doesn't make it not so," Luna said. She repeated the line in her head, the one she had been told by her parents for as long as she could remember: *Home can be anywhere. Home is what you make it.* Her life hadn't always felt very stable, with so much of it spent on the road. She thought of herself as a seed blown on the wind, while other kids had roots. When she was younger, trips with Big Bear sometimes meant missed birthday parties, or growing distant from friends, and she had envied those kids with roots.

But as she got older, she realized not everyone got to skip around different continents and dip their feet in multiple oceans. Maybe she didn't have a normal home, but the idea of *Home can be anywhere* was a reminder that 'not normal' didn't mean 'less than.' In fact, she was pretty sure it was 'more than'—more special, more meaningful—than sticking around in one place, and just now, Luna couldn't figure out why her dad seemed to be arguing *against* it.

Big Bear let out a long breath. "Sure. Home can be anywhere. But you gotta let people decide where the 'where' is. You don't get to tell them."

"Ah," Luna said, and she smiled. "So you're saying don't get in the way of someone? Let them go where they want to go?"

"If they're an *adult*, sure. Parents get to order their kids around."

Now they were driving right by the mill, a sprawling complex that took up the space of a small town. The person Big Bear needed to interview worked at a building that was further up the road, at the edge of the mill property. The car lurched ahead, but after a few minutes they stopped again.

Luna looked outside the window at smoke-stained concrete and faded brick and asphalt. She saw nothing that looked alive, or like it had ever been alive, except for the dark, dead stacks of trees. Opposite the building was a few acres of mud, lorded over by a sign that cheerfully proclaimed, amidst the muck and piles of gravel: "Facility expansion: coming soon!"

A man in an orange vest walked over and told Big Bear and Luna to stretch their legs; a truck had broken down up ahead and it was blocking traffic. Other cars and trucks were stopped, and the mill workers who were driving them had gotten out to stretch and, appropriately enough, mill around.

Luna and her dad left their own car, and Big Bear struck up a conversation with a group of men leaning against the hood of a pick-up.

"Are we gonna be here for a while?" Luna asked, loud enough for the men to hear.

One of them nodded to Big Bear. "At least another half hour, I'd say. Probably longer."

"Can I walk around?" Luna asked.

Her dad sighed but nodded. "Don't wander too far," he said, but she was already gone.

When Luna wandered into the fog she had been frightened by its mystery. She felt just as unsettled here, but for a different reason. This place looked shattered. She walked to the edge of the mud field and gazed on a patch of yellow-brown dirt gone slimy from rain, dotted with scummy pools of water. Splinters of wood lay in the mire, soggy and sharp, jutting from the earth like venomous teeth.

In the middle of the mud a hump of wood, brush, and leftover leaves rotted into a mass the size of a car. Luna knew the word for that tangle was a 'deadfall,' which was, she realized, its own sort of kenning. She wondered how the look of the deadfall so perfectly fit the word it described: there had been a forest, and animals, and life, and now this. Broken branches. Brown pine needles. Leaves gone so soft they were slime. And . . .

. . . something else. Wet, and dark. A shadow of a claw?

Luna's heart caught. Something slender and sharp stretched out from beneath a log. It gently scratched at the air, beckoning her forward, like spider's legs dancing across a web.

She could still see her dad, talking to the workers. She thought of Gordon's stories of following Things into the woods. Her heart beat faster; Luna was on her own. Her dad wasn't paying attention. He couldn't tell her what was safe, or what was her heart's desire.

She walked towards the deadfall. Mud squished around her sneakers, and the beginning of damp cold pressed on her feet.

Luna looked back; Big Bear was a dozen metres away, still talking with the man in the vest. She pushed on, right to the edge of the deadfall, and two ravens flew above her, perching on the broken bodies of the trees. They stared at Luna and croaked a song, and then, as if it were moving in time with their music, the land around her came *undone*. It was as if the world had become an origami sculpture that was rapidly unfolding. The sky flipped over the horizon; the few standing trees bent in on themselves like they were creased right down the middle. The deadfall itself ripped in half, and fog rushed in to fill the gaps where there had been rotting wood just moments before.

The ravens finished their song: *quork quork*.

Luna felt her body slip past the mists at the lip of the deadfall, and then she heard nothing more.

4

Luna could not see her dad, nor the road, nor the construction crews. She was, she realized, somewhere *else*. In this case, the 'else' was the forest, or at least, *a* forest. This was not the clearcut she had been standing in. No trees had been felled here in years, if ever. There were leaves, and roots, and vines.

But there were no people, or even the signs of people, anywhere.

The juices in her guts begin to boil with anxiety, and she took deep breaths to steady herself.

OK, Luna thought. *Guess I'm in a magic woods. If a weird thing beckons at you from a deadfall and you end up in woods and the world unfolds, then they're definitely magic woods. That's how it works.*

And since she was in a magic woods, she wasn't going to sit around and wait for something to happen. People who did that in stories did not make it to the end of them. No, Luna would walk. Only days ago, she had looked out over the cliff, wanting a little danger. Well, she was sure there was danger in this forest (because what enchanted forest *wasn't* dangerous?), and she meant to find it, rather than the other way around.

As she walked, Luna took in her surroundings. And the more she looked, the more she realized she might have been mistaken about how *alive* this place was. There were trees, yes, far more than had been in the clearcut. Mainly larch and spruce, and what she thought were maples sprinkled throughout. But they were *wrong*. The bark was scaly, and in places it had been stripped away, leaving bone white trunks bleeding sticky red sap. No tree seemed to have reached their full height. Instead, they hunched over, like they resented the idea of growing tall. Luna did not touch the trees, but it was impossible not to brush against the undergrowth, mainly vines and creepers, thick and tangled.

Dad had told her too much undergrowth was the sign of a sick forest. Here, the bracken was a snarled carpet.

Her throat was tight with tension. She needed air. So she inhaled deeply—and immediately retched. The air reeked of foulness, the stink around the paper mill multiplied and magnified into a wave of chemical, ash, and decay that made Luna ill right in her guts. Now she moved with two goals in mind: finding whatever it was that had beckoned her into the woods and moving away from this rotten egg air—quickly.

She picked up her pace and kept walking—she wasn't sure what direction, just away from where she was. But the earth went from cold and hard to soft and yielding, and soon her feet became stuck. Mud was gripping her sneakers. But after she looked up from freeing her feet, the broken trees had knotted into a half-deadfall, a fence of thorns and bracken. Water seemed to be everywhere, but it was oily and dark, laced with greasy bubbles that pooled on the surface of puddles that pockmarked the forest floor. She kept moving, around the thorny fence, now moving slowly, *slurrrrping* her feet from the mud every few steps, and it did not take long for her feet to become soaked.

Where are the birds? she wondered. Their music might lead her out of this desperate place since no living thing would choose to stay here. But Luna heard no cheeps, caws, or croaks, or the high *yip* of Gordon's osprey. Only the air, moving through the trees with a soft, insistent *hiss*.

The sun was gone, although it wasn't night. Instead, a dark grey cloudbank—*or maybe*, Luna thought, *it's the smoke of the mill. So strong I can see and smell it, even in the magic woods*—covered the sky. A deep, cold wet infused the air. This was a sick place, and that became a kenning: the *sick smoke*.

A cold panic tightened Luna's chest, and she began to move more quickly, careful to only breathe through her mouth. The air still left a sour, metallic taste on her tongue, but she could stomach that compared to the scent of the sick smoke.

The red-sap trees waved their branches like bone fingers. On the ground, piles of rotten bark glistened. A few feet away, a carpet of glistening mushrooms, pale as the moon. A faint fuzz spread across their bulbous caps, which glowed a nauseous green grey. She turned away, and the moment she did she noticed the barest glimmer of movement out of the corner of her eye. When she swivelled her head back, the mushrooms had edged closer.

Luna froze. Tears began to form in her eyes. Angrily, she brushed them away and began walking again. There was nothing wrong with being scared, she told herself, but she could not let her fear freeze her in one place.

She began to run—again, in what direction she wasn't sure, but away from the mushrooms and the stink seemed like a good start. She tore through the woods, those twisted, bleeding, scaly, *wrong* woods, as fast her feet could carry her, her shoes digging into the ground, the leaves pressing onto her jeans like gently scratching claws.

That was when she almost stepped on the fox.

It lay still, in the leaves, and looked as sick as the trees, if not sicker. More bones than fur, and what fur was left was dirty, clumped with black soil and leaves.

The fox raised its head weakly and looked at her. Its eyes were misted, and its teeth were yellow. It made no noise, but its eyes seemed to scream, *Water. Please.*

In the distance, Luna saw the mushrooms: creeping, growing, spreading fungal tentacles like landbound jellyfish. She tried to ignore them and focus on the fox. She felt sorry for it, and absolutely did not want to get closer to it. One of her mother's first rules for the outdoors was to never touch wildlife. That went double if the animal looked sick. This animal was very sick, and whatever made it sick could jump onto her. Part of her thought she should let it die. Maybe the truly kind thing to do was end the fox's pain, although Luna didn't know how to do that, or if she could.

But another part of her whispered, *The rules in a regular forest don't work in this one.* And as soon as that whisper finished, Luna took a water bottle out of her backpack and knelt by the fox.

The poor creature barely moved as she approached it, but it did tilt its head back and open its jaws. Luna poured a trickle of water into its mouth. Water dribbled onto the animal's neck and the cold ground, but most of it ran down its throat.

Luna wasn't sure what would happen now. She knew what she *wanted* to happen. The fox would sit up with its eyes aglow, lick its chops and speak in a funny voice—"Oh, why thank you ever so much my newfound friend,"—and then show her the way home.

That didn't happen. The fox's eyes brightened for a moment. Then they narrowed and dimmed. The animal licked its nose once with a rough, brown tongue. Its breathing slowed, its sides puffing and retracting, but growing slower, and slower, until they reached the edge of stillness.

Luna made herself watch the fox take its last breath.

She cried. She wasn't sure why. She had seen something die, and that felt important. She hoped wherever the fox was, if it was anywhere, it was a better place than the sick smoke. It had to be.

The *wahks* and *quorks* began not long after, followed by a rush of wings. A half dozen ravens flapped down and hopped towards the fox's body. Luna wanted to scream and chase them away. She didn't want them to disturb the fox's body. But she knew that sort of thing didn't matter to other animals. They didn't think in terms of good or evil, or polite and rude—they just lived, or died, or fed, or hungered. These birds were doing what they had to do, and that was eating the dead.

Besides: the mushrooms had been growing, spreading, *moving* towards Luna, like a slow, pallid amoeba. But when the black birds landed, desperate for their carrion feast, the mushroom field stopped. It even seemed to recede, back into the dark spaces between fallen logs and mouldering leaves.

The birds began to peck at the fox. Luna turned away. But then, she heard one raven, croaking and gurgling, louder than the rest. No, two ravens, both screaming in a way that was quite *insistent*.

Luna looked back toward them and quickly sucked in her breath. The fox was gone—completely gone, leaving no trace of bones or fur. In its place was a single stone that could fit in the palm of her hand, dark and flecked with silvery mica, like a piece of a starry night sky that had fallen to Earth.

Luna read stories. She knew stones like this did not appear without reason.

She picked it up. The stone felt as smooth as a marble, but otherwise, ordinary.

Wahk. Wahk wahk wahk.

The two ravens that fed on the fox were staring at her now. Their feathers shone bright and black, even in the half light, and their eyes were as cold and sharp as their dagger beaks.

"What do you want?" Luna asked, as she pocketed the stone in the pouch of her hoodie. And the birds cocked their heads to the side in a way that was almost cute, like they were curious puppies, instead of scavengers that could carve the flesh off a skeleton.

The closest raven opened its beak and went, *Wahk wahk wAAaahk whaddawahn*. It almost sounded like it was repeating what Luna had said: "What do you want?" But that was silly, because birds can't talk. They could gesture, though, and the two ravens did a sort of dance, with hops and flaps, a dance that said, *Follow us*.

Following two birds that popped out of nowhere is kind of a silly thing to do, she thought. Then she thought of the choking air, the sopping ground, and alien mushrooms.

She followed the ravens.

The birds went slow, stopping here and there to perch on a branch and raise their black wings, so they looked like feathered capes. Sometimes, they would look at Luna, and then they would sing, scratchy and rough, a chorus that urged Luna on, scolded her when she slowed, and always echoed in her skull: *whaddawahn whaddawahn whaddawahn.*

She followed the ravens for so long she lost all sense of how much time had passed—maybe half an hour, maybe half a day, maybe half a year. But the forest was changing. At first the ground had been muddy and moist, relentlessly soft under her feet. But as she walked further, the squishing sound was gradually replaced by something crisper, and less quiet: the satisfying crunch of dead leaves. Dead, *dry* leaves, not the mouldy floor of the sick smoke. Luna wasn't sure where she was now, but it was a better place than where she had been.

She took a moment to stop, breathe, collect herself, and look around. The ravens were gone. They had led her to a place where the trees were healthy and strong, their roots spreading amidst good, black soil under pillows of soft, wet moss. She opened her ears, and what she heard was silence: deep, all-encompassing, and *green.* She'd never known noise, or the absence of noise, could have colour, but she'd never been in a forest like this, either.

She had looked and listened; now she decided to sniff. And what she smelled was woods, wet, and winter. It was the smell of frost that had yet to break, ready to rear its icy head without permission. Luna could almost taste the cold air, and it was wonderful. She decided to walk in the direction where the cold smell was strongest.

Soon the scent was so thick it seemed to lend the air weight. In between some of the tree trunks there was—not a fog, or a cloud—but *something*, soft and transparent as a dragonfly's wing. It was less a colour than the impression of it. Luna made a kenning: *green mist*. Even that kenning did not quite seize the shape of it, because this mist did not spread through all the woods so much as point in a direction, like a thread she could follow through a maze, just like in the tale of Theseus fighting the minotaur.

That was one of her favourite stories, because Theseus wasn't forced into the labyrinth. He was a prince. He could have lived the rest of his life in comfort at the palace, eating grapes and olives and watching the sun set into the sea every day. But that was not Theseus's way. No: when his city was threatened by the minotaur, he volunteered to sail to Crete and enter the monster's labyrinth. He was clever and used a thread to find his way through the maze, but when the time came, he was brave, ready to fight when he had no other choice. Of course, Theseus ended up betraying Ariadne, the princess who helped him, and when he sailed home to Athens, he forgot to set the correctly coloured sails on his boat. As a result, his father thought Theseus had died, and became so sad he . . .

Well, Luna hated that part of the story. She preferred to focus on how Theseus had used his wits and courage to beat a monster. The other stuff was just depressing.

She pushed those details out of her mind. Right now, she had to be like Theseus. He sought out danger and conquered it. She chose to enter this place, and now she was going to survive it—and maybe, defeat the minotaur that lurked within.

Whatever that may be, she thought.

She looked at the forest floor, black and boggy, and saw two rows of crescent moon arcs. *Hoofprints*, she thought. Then she heard a flapping above her. The ravens sat, preening in a branch as gnarled as an old man's tooth. They stared at Luna long and hard, like they were expecting a show. She stared right back at them, wondering what they found so interesting about her, until she got tired of doing so and dropped her gaze and looked in front of her, and that was when she saw the Thing.

5

It—*no*, thought Luna, *He*—wasn't very tall, but from the top of his head to his strange hairy legs he was all muscle, whip lean and wire strong. His skin was dark and gnarled, like bark left in the rain. He had a long beard matted with leaves, twigs, and bracken, which barely but not quite concealed a smile that wrinkled his face into a walnut shell of creases. Past the wrinkles Luna saw warm and friendly eyes. She thought, *Oh. He looks nice.*

Then she *really* looked at the eyes. Wandered into them for a moment that stretched too long for her comfort. And those eyes weren't just warm. They were *hot*. Embers plucked from a fire.

Luna's mom told her once that behind the eyes you can see the heart. There, in the forest, under the ravens and the twisted tree, she looked beyond this Thing's eyes, and saw no kind of heart worth knowing. Instead, there was hunger, open and enormous, an appetite like an out-of-control furnace. It was the kind of hunger that devours forests and, maybe, a child.

She heard herself breathing, very fast, very loud. Fear had scooped out a part of her insides and filled them with icy water. The cold threatened to numb her, paralyze her with panic and anxiety.

Stop this, Luna told herself. *I wanted a quest. To find danger. To see monsters. I can't turn around now that one has shown up.* She pushed against her inner chill with hot determination.

After all, Luna thought, *he is little*. Just a little over her height. And he just sat there, a small Thing in a dirty shirt on a root as thick as a log, his legs tucked under the brush so you couldn't see his feet.

Then the Thing began tapping on the root with double jointed, crooked fingers, capped with sharp nails. And he grinned, and his mouth was full of daggers.

Frozen water poured into Luna's stomach again.

"We meet again, little moon," the Thing said. His voice sounded like the wind in the trees on a cold night. "Hello and welcome to the Heart of the Forest. My name is Billy."

"What do you mean, 'again?'" Luna asked. "And how do you know my name?" She didn't like that Billy said 'little moon,' her dad's nickname for her, like he was describing an after-dinner treat.

Billy leaned forward. She could see the fur on his legs more clearly. Like his beard, they were matted with dirt and mud, twigs and pine needles that gummed to him like a second skin.

"I know everyone who comes into my woods," Billy said.

"*Your* woods?" Luna asked.

"Well, my name isn't on them. But I've left my mark, just the same."

He's as arrogant as he looks, Luna thought. She decided to keep Billy talking. She had a feeling that doing so wouldn't be difficult. She'd read a lot of fairy tales. Things that thought they owned something as un-ownable as a forest liked to talk, and what they liked to talk about most was themselves.

And the more he talks, Luna thought, *the less time he has to eat. And that's good, because I think I know what would be on the menu.*

She swallowed a lump of her nerves. They tasted like sick.

"Have these always been your woods?" she asked.

"A part of them, yes," said Billy. "The far part. The edges. I can tell you all about it." A sharp red tongue emerged from his mouth as he licked lips riddled with cracks and sores.

Luna nodded, even as she tried to ignore Billy's mouth.

"Go on," she said. "Please. Tell me all about the edges."

Billy laughed, high and hollow. "A story it is then, my girl. A Once Upon a Time."

Luna had a feeling this story would be ugly, but she listened, hoping Billy would give up a weapon she could use in what was shaping up to be a battle of wits.

"Once upon a time," Billy said, slowly, as if he were relishing each word, "Billy lived where the leaves and the mud are black as midnight. He snuck about where white grubs eat soft logs, and nettles grow in the deadfalls. Aye, that was where Billy took his tea. That was the good forest, hale and healthy."

"It doesn't sound very healthy," Luna said.

"Because there was rot? What smells rotten to you is sweet to me, for that was Billy's job: to stoke the rot. To keep things dyin', so as to make room for more things livin'. But then . . . you people came. I woke up one morning, and where once was a grove, there was mud. Thickets turned thin. Copses became corpses, clear cut, cut clean away. I had nothing left to rot, for nothing was left alive. The tree spaces and leaf places had grown cold and wet, and nothing grew in them but a foul scent."

The sick smoke, Luna thought, and the thought must have been written clear across her face, because Billy grinned and said, "Yes, child. I think you've been there. I think you've smelled the rank air. Seen the stiff trees. Walked a land gone barren and bitter. I think you know that place quite well."

"Is that why you're here?" Luna asked. "To fight the sick smoke? To bring the forest back to what it was?" She almost felt sorry for Billy. She wondered: if the sick smoke had hurt her, maybe it hurt Billy too? It sounded like Billy was the rot in a dance of life and death, a dance that was as much a part of nature as pretty leaves and red foxes. And now that dance was broken by the smokestacks, and the dying ground, and the bad air.

But then Billy raised a claw to its mouth and picked something dark and squirming from between his long teeth: a beetle. "You mistake my meaning, girl. Once, I served the rot. Serve the rot, serve the forest. But no longer. I *like* what the woods have become. What you call 'sick smoke,' I call 'fresh air.'"

Luna felt her jaw drop. "Who do you serve now then?" she asked. But Billy just grinned at her, his pointed teeth bared, as he ignored her question.

"I'll tell you something. My feet have been restless, little Luna," he went on, and when he said 'feet' he tucked his legs in more, as if to keep her attention away from them, "so I have moved myself from the smelly places and their rotten water. Now I make a new home, where I can feast and entertain my friends. Right here, at the Heart of the Forest."

He gestured at a bent tree that grew over his shoulder. It seemed not much different than a hundred other trees—a medium-height pine tree, slender and strong. But the more Luna stared at it, the more twisted it seemed, like the branches had tied themselves into a sailor's knot. Under her gaze the tree seemed to breathe.

Billy idly began scratching a deep gouge into the root he sat on, and when he did, the air in the glen shuddered and the trees—not any one tree, but *all* of them—wilted a little like a flower suddenly exposed to a blast of intense heat.

That root is part of the bent tree, Luna thought. *And the bent tree is part of . . . all the trees.*

She had been so focused on Billy she had lost sight of the forest that surrounded him, but now it came into focus. The root Billy sat on could have been the bark-clad tentacle of a giant squid, but the ground was *full* of roots, some as thick as the tentacle log, some thin as a branch, and others of all sizes in between, all growing out of and into the soil, where they wove together like a living cloak. Every plant in this forest had roots, of course, but they all grew from *these* roots. And what happened to these roots would spread to anything they touched—which was everything.

Billy watched her and winked. "I like this chat. Been many moons since I met a moon so pleasant to talk with." He laughed again, ice cracking on a cold river. "So I ask: will you be my friend, Luna? For what is a friend, but a stranger you now know by name? And name to name, you and I are *quite* acquainted."

He smiled again, and against her better judgement

(and with a small degree of shock), Luna smiled back. She wasn't sure why. She was pretending to be pleasant, yes, because that felt like the smart move when dealing with a hungry monster, but a part of her was also, truly, enchanted: sitting in this magic place with this magic creature, in a strange, silent corner of a forest that stretched as far and wide as Billy's smile.

Luna made herself look at the edges of that smile. Really look. There, the wrinkled, tree bark skin was beginning to crack, and she thought she could see things crawling beneath: more beetles, and centipedes, and other things with shiny carapaces and clacking legs.

Big smile, big appetite, Luna thought.

"You're sitting silent, girl," Billy drawled, the words practically dripping from his mouth. "Maybe you're scared to speak to me. But is the scared in you, little Luna? Or does it come from your dull, doting daddy?"

Billy's eye glinted with delight and malevolence, but the mention of her father made Luna's stomach twist, her cheeks blush. Then she saw Billy's eyes flash redder, hotter. *He's trying to make me angry*, she thought. *Because the angrier I get, the less clever I am . . .*

Then she remembered a lesson her dad told her: if you're trying to win an argument, ask the other person questions about their ideas. If they can't answer, you've got them in a corner. Asking questions always came easy to Luna. Now she let her questions fill the forest, even as she wondered how to escape it.

"I don't understand why you're here, Billy." Luna said. "You sound like you enjoy your smelly place and the dirty water. Why leave that for this?" She gestured all around. The *this* they stood in was green and growing, tangled and wild and, above all, beautiful, so unlike the cold, choking chill of the sick smoke.

"Oh, Luna. I like *this*. I like this so I can make it more like *that*." Billy pointed at the mud sludging near the log he sat on. "Don't forget, I come from the rotten parts, Luna. I might not serve the rot anymore, but the rot is in me. It follows me. And rot likes to *move*. To spread. I brought it here, very much on purpose. Do you think that's a bad thing?" he cooed. "It's just the way the woods work. No point in keeping the rot in a place that's already dead. New things don't grow until old things die. The forest is born in the cool, black soil, and it's the rot that feeds it. You'll find more animals in a dead log than a live tree. Not that I love the living trees. This'd be a land of icy mud and maggots if I had my way."

"So, I was right," Luna said, half to Billy and half to herself, "when I told my dad that the mill and those loggers were bad for this place. They chopped down the trees, and hurt the land, and that's what brought you out."

There was a noise that landed somewhere between a hacking cough and a rabid dog's bark. Luna realized Billy was laughing.

"HA! Ah, girl, you're as set in your thoughts as any rock in a mountain," he said. He rapped his fist on a nearby boulder. "No, Luna. The one who cuts the tree does so for their family. People have taken wood from the woods for years. Taken fish out the ocean or deer for their table since they rubbed two flints together to make a fire. Trees have been cut here for hundreds of years, but the act of felling them didn't bring me here."

"Then what did?"

Billy cocked his head. "I brought me here." As he said the next few words, he paused every so often to drum on the log with his sharp fingers. "All." *Thump.* "By." *Thwick.* "My." *Thwap.* "Self." The fire in his eyes grew bloodier. "Because I am Billy. I am the hunger of those with a full stomach who want more food. The craving of them with a full pocket that still steal. I am *desire*: the need to see a thing and *have* it. I know the truth of possession: what you win is yours and yours alone, and those that ask you to share only envy your strength.

"*That* is why I am here, little moon. I bring rot, but I crave *life*, so I may corrupt it to my ends and chew it for my supper. One lovely, dark day, I sniffed out the Heart of the Forest, the heartbeat of the island. I *sniffed* it, and I *took* it, and oh what I *found* and have *ground* between my gums. There is so much *life* here, and I will gnaw at it. Sharpen my teeth on it. Suck its marrow forever." He paused and blew a low whistle as he fixed Luna with his fiery red eyes. "And maybe have a snack on the side."

Luna imagined just how wide Billy's appetite could stretch. She had a feeling there was no limit.

He said it himself, she thought. *He's a hungry Thing and can never be full. And if he had his way, this would be a land of icy mud and maggots.*

Those words were terrible, but the memory of them steadied Luna. Her quest was clear. She would not let Billy have his way.

She kept breathing, low and slow, trying to channel her thoughts, to turn the fear of being trapped into the hope of escape. Then, as if the thought had been there since she first walked into Billy's mud-and-loam audience hall and just needed to be dusted off, she had an idea: of how to leave that place, and maybe banish Billy too.

Luna's hand drifted to her hoodie's pocket. She squeezed the stone she had picked up earlier, the stone like a night sky that came from the place where the fox died after its thirst was slaked. Above her, in the trees, the ravens babbled with scratchy excitement.

Quork. Quork.

"Well, I've enjoyed talking with you, Billy," Luna said. Oddly enough, she meant it. Billy's voice was cold, his teeth were too long, but he was *charming*, from the tips of his greasy hair to the ends of his dirty fingernails.

"But I'm not sure I can stay," she added.

Billy's eyes flared, and he scratched more furrows into the log. "But you must! You must stay and have some food. Eat, eat, *eat*. Eat with me Luna. I set a table where the feast doesn't end."

Who's on the menu? Luna thought, and her eyes narrowed. *Him*, she decided.

"I have to be on my way," Luna went on. "But if you're hungry, I have this nice bit of cheese. It's my last piece. All I have left, but I don't mind sharing."

Billy giggled, high and mocking, the way a bully might before they say something cruel. "Oh yes. Cheese if you please."

He held out his long, crooked fingers, caked with dirt. Another kenning spun a new web in Luna's head: *spider knuckles*.

Luna took the stone out of her hoodie, carefully keeping it covered with her hand.

Billy slowly drew nearer. His breath smelled of old leaves left for too long on the forest floor. Luna's fear rose in her throat, but just then the stone felt harder, very hard, like it had taken on an extra measure of *stoniness*.

Suddenly, Billy's arms snapped out and he snatched the stone from her fist. He raised the rock to his mouth, his sharp teeth, so greedy he didn't look on what he stuffed into his jaws.

Luna watched Billy's grin, and she watched it shatter,

along with his teeth.

Thick, foul liquid spilled out of Billy's mouth, an eruption of tarry black sludge, followed by rotting incisors and molars. The little demon fell to the earth, screaming in agony, then spun on his hooves and turned on her.

"Wicked girl!" he cried, but the words barely escaped his muffled mouth. "You've broken my jaws!" He howled in pain.

"How can I gnaw and nibble the Heart of the Forest now!" Billy screamed. And then he leapt away, on furry legs that ended in mud-caked hooves, back to the edge of the woods where the water runs black and the mud is thick, and then past that, to where the trees were dead and the sick smoke hung over everything.

The stone lay on the ground. It was still smooth, despite Billy's bite. Next to it lay teeth, crooked and brown.

A raven flapped onto the branch of the bent tree, the one all the roots grew from. The wood of that tree was twisted, old, and moss green. Luna saw scratches all across its bark. The wounds looked angry, like they were infected. They had been dug with crooked teeth and dirty claws.

"Is this the tree Billy called the Heart of the Forest?" Luna wondered aloud, remembering Billy's story. The raven did not answer, because that would be silly, because birds don't talk. But it did tilt its head to the side, and it pecked a neighbouring branch.

Luna came closer, sucked her breath in quickly, reached out, and touched the tree.

Suddenly, her body was filled with forest. First, her toes become roots, and her arms, branches, and she, Luna, was a tree, and not just *a* tree but all trees, touching every leaf and root on the island at the same time, like she held a little bit of all the life of the land. It was not exactly a *good* feeling, but neither was it bad. Rather, it was *full*, and powerful, and rich, like every cell of hers was growing and groaning with immense force.

Luna pulled her hand away from the ancient tree, and the full forest feeling drifted away, like a dream that dissolves just slow enough to feel bittersweet.

I was the forest just now, Luna thought. It had been a big feeling, huge as an ancient maple and light as the thinnest pine needle all at once. It was too much—she thought if she touched the tree again, she might never let go of it, but maybe that would not be the worst thing: to stay there, forever, growing into the forest.

But she knew she had a life to go back to. And the thought of returning to that life after this first quest, this first major victory, swelled her heart.

I got lost in magic woods where the air was poison, but it didn't matter, because I found my own way out and faced off against some hungry monster in its lair and I BEAT it and then I touched that tree and I became the forest. I did all that.

All. By. My. Self.

She laughed. Pride swelled in her heart, and it felt *good*. Luna breathed in deeply, and the smell was the first day of spring after a long, hard winter.

She laughed again. *I deserve a little piece of these woods*, came a thought. *I just saved this tree from the Thing that wanted to devour it. Which means a part of it belongs to me. I can take it home.*

There, above the root, on a low-hanging branch that grew out of the bent tree, was a pinecone, whiteish and damp and flecked with green. It was alone on the branch, which swayed, gently and slowly, in a wind that didn't move any of the other branches.

In the woods, by herself, Luna sometimes talked to her mom. Now she thought of her. The hellraiser. Wild as a storm. She did what she wanted, when she wanted. No demons or dads stood in her way.

The pinecone spun, like a living prize.

Quick as fire, too fast for her heart to object, Luna grabbed it. The moment she touched it that feeling of being *full* returned, but then the pinecone broke off the tree with a crisp *snap* and . . . Luna gasped. The feeling was gone, sucked out of her like water down a drain. She had to grab at the root Billy had sat on to keep herself from falling into the cold mud.

Luna looked at the pinecone: hard, spiky, oddly

heavy. A piece of the Heart of the Forest. She bent her face towards it and inhaled. It had the Christmas smell of Gordon's house, but *more*, heavier with everything that made that scent distinct—wood, green needles, lichen, *life*.

But when she looked at the branch where she'd snapped the cone from the tree, her heart jumped a little. There was a tiny blotch there, and it glittered, wet and dark. Slowly, she ran a finger over the discolouration. There was no feeling of becoming a forest. She pressed on the tree trunk. The wood gave a little. Like it had gone rotten.

It was very quiet in the woods. But Luna's thoughts echoed in her mind: *why would you hurt the forest you said you saved why would you hurt it why would you why why why.*

She tried to brush these echoes away. *I am Luna. I'm a hellraiser that fights monsters from hell, and I haven't done anything wrong,* she told herself. *Big Bear isn't here to tell me otherwise.*

She forced herself to smile.

But then the ravens, who had moved their perches to the upper branches of the bent tree, began cawing uncontrollably. Their croaks had shifted from *whaddyawan* to *whydja whydja whydja*. They sounded like an accusation, underlined by the way they now *stared* at Luna. The more she tried to ignore their rasping, the louder it grew.

"Just . . . *shut up*," Luna said, loudly. And immediately, the ravens went silent, although they never broke their slow, hard stare. She met their winter eyes with her green ones, then put the pinecone in her backpack.

"It's *mine*," she said. "I beat Billy. I won it. I earned it," she said.

One of the ravens puffed its throat feathers. The other hopped, briefly, on a branch.

"Mine," Luna repeated. "And now I am going."

She thought about saying 'goodbye,' and decided not to. Instead, she walked, with no direction in mind, just away. She was *meant* to fight Billy. Now that the fight was over, her time on this side of the deadfall was done. That pile of branches and rot had been the door here; now she needed to find the way back, to her dad, and the car, and everything that entailed. Except there were no directions in this forest. It was a confusing place, but she knew one thing: wherever she needed to be, it was not *here*.

Indeed, the more she walked, the more she started to hear sounds from the forest, but not *this* forest of croaking ravens and goat-legged tricksters. She heard the music of normal woods: chirps, scritches, scratches, twigs cracking, leaves rustling.

After a few more minutes Luna heard the *whuzz* of engines and smelled the stale blacktop scent of a road. The trees were thinning, and soon she emerged from the woods into a deadfall, which stood in a mud patch, which was across from the car where her dad stood chatting with construction and lumber workers. She wasn't sure how long she had been gone—hours?—but she fully expected to come back to a scene of chaos, of workers and police searching for her and her dad panicking (which even Luna had to admit would have been understandable).

Instead, he was speaking with the same workers he had been chatting with when she left, and he looked bored.

He turned towards his daughter, frowning.

"Jeez, kid, I turn my head away for a minute and you look like you got in the middle of a fight between a mudslide and a thornbush."

"A . . . minute?" Luna asked.

"If that."

Luna was decent at making excuses for her long absences—she had even thought of a kenning for them ever since coming to Newfoundland: *gone songs*. But she didn't need one now. However long she had been gone, the world remained as it was, except she had left it, and defeated a demon, and won a piece of the Heart of the Forest.

"Sorry Dad," Luna said. "Just poking around."

"Bad idea, miss," said one of the lumber workers. "It's real easy to hurt yourself in these trees." Then he looked confused, as Luna's laughter rang out under the overcast sky.

6

Luna had entered a magic forest and faced off with a hungry goat-legged monster, and this put her in an uncommonly bright mood. As Big Bear drove her away from the mill, she even stopped complaining about the smell. That evening, she did not drag her heels when it came time to set the table for dinner. Luna, vanquisher of Billy, wasn't going to get into a fight over what side of the plate the water glass went on.

"I know, the right side, Daaaad," she said, walking quickly through the kitchen and giggling. Big Bear looked at her as she sailed into and out of the room. She poked her head back in to see her dad glance at Gordon, who gave a shrug. Luna had developed a masterful literacy when it came to reading adult gestures, and she was pretty sure that one said, in the silent language of parents, "I don't know, and neither will you."

A few minutes later she sat down to dinner with her dad and Gordon and dug into a plate of fried fish and hot chips—a dinner made of nuggets of scalding gold. When the plates were empty and their bellies were full, Gordon brewed some coffee and began to talk about the old days.

Luna was in a good mood already, and the lightness of her heart only grew as Gordon, a natural tale teller, launched into his stories: about the days when everyone fished for work and hunted sea birds that were so oily, they floated on the waves for a day after you shot them, and instead of a fridge, families put their food in cellars cut out of the turf that stayed cold on the hottest summer day.

Then, when the night was truly alive and the dark seemed to sneak under the door—*like a 'shadow thief,'* Luna thought—Gordon talked about monsters, and faeries, and ghosts.

Big Bear shifted to the edge of his chair. "Do you think there are ghosts here?" he asked.

Luna's ears perked. Her backpack was under the table. She quietly unzipped it and put her hands on the pinecone inside of it, a pinecone snapped off a tree that bore the scratch and bite marks of a monster with an appetite that could swallow the world.

Gordon nodded. "This is an old island with long memories. Many of our people came from Ireland and brought banshees with them: spirits of women crying for something they lost in life. They haunt empty places, and try to fill that void with their voices, but folks say their screams will steal the soul out of your skin."

Luna could see Big Bear's eyes flash with excitement. They both loved watching horror movies on his laptop while cuddled together in bed. When she looked at him, their eyes caught each other, and his beard cracked into a smile. The room seemed to warm up. She hadn't realized how much she missed him.

"Anyways," Gordon went on, "We got ghosts here, yes, but we also have ghost *towns*."

"*Real* ghost towns?" Luna asked.

"Oh yes. Did you know the house I grew up in is still there, walls and all, but empty? One day men from the government told us our community was in a bad way: too poor, too far from schools and hospitals, too cut off from the world. That was news to us, seeing as there were still fish in the sea and bread in our ovens. But the men told us we had to live in new homes in another part of the island, so we left the houses our fathers' fathers built, and the cellars our mothers' mothers stocked, and now they all sit empty. Or it may seem like that. There are a lot of empty towns on this rock. And I think the land there remembers."

Luna thought of how angry she got when her dad told her not to go somewhere for her own good, then imagined how mad she would be if someone told her where to *live*. Gordon, in the meantime, had gone silent. He looked far away, like he was sitting in a quiet corner of his head.

Big Bear leaned forward and asked, "You used to fish, right Gordon? Do you miss it?"

The old man's eyes swam through oceans of memory back into his kitchen. "It was bitter hard work with no damn hope for anything but smelling like cod guts at the end of the day," he said. "Always a fight between you and the water. All pain, and precious little gain." He sighed through his nose; his old storytelling rhythm had returned.

"But I loved it. It was our life, and we lived it to the bone. Then the factory ships came and sucked the fish up, so now even the baby cod can't grow up because their parents aren't there to eat the things that eat them. When that happened, I took my family, left the island, and moved across the country to a place where I built homes for people who made fun of the way I talk. It was a flat, dry place, and the only ocean was made of grass."

"It sounds awful," said Luna.

"It was," said Gordon. "But the work put a roof over my kids' heads, and the money was good. My own daughter was born here, grew up smelling the fish on these docks, but she ended up staying out west, because that's where the work is. And anyways, this place had lots of hard memories. People lost jobs. Some of them lost their minds." He paused, and Luna saw he had gone back to the quiet corner of his mind. "Some lost more than that. There are lots of ghosts here, Luna. Being around the memories of the dead can be as haunting as a spirit itself."

Big Bear nodded, silently.

"So why did you come back?" Luna asked.

Gordon shrugged. "Well, for one, I got to an age where I started getting a pension, which is money the government gives old people for not being dead. And not long after I retired, my wife passed away, and . . . I wanted to be in the place that reminded me of her. But *also*, I realized something, out there on those plains and prairies: as many hard memories were here, this place—this island, this house we're sitting in, that my father and uncles built together—this is my *home*."

Gordon sat back, smiling. Her dad was nodding, his face (the kenning came to her) a *feelings-map* of sympathy and understanding. Gordon nodded at her father, then looked at Luna. Clearly, he expected her to feel the same way as Big Bear. Luna wondered if he had told this story to other guests before, and they had all showed the same *feelings-map* Big Bear was wearing, claiming sympathy for his exile, and satisfaction that he had come back.

Luna shook her head.

"This is a house," she said. "If you think about it, a house is just walls and a roof. A home doesn't have to be a house, though. Home can be anywhere. Home is what you make it. That's what my parents told me."

She *was* quoting her mom. *And* Big Bear. She thought of Gordon as a good friend and wanted to comfort him, let him know he could feel at 'home,' feel like he was where he was supposed to be, without being in one particular place. That was how she had always lived her life. But her dad was frowning and subtly shaking his head.

Gordon looked taken aback. Maybe, Luna thought, he wasn't used to being challenged by children. She grinned a little inside; long debates with her dad made her unafraid of challenging adults.

Gordon collected himself. "You're not wrong, Luna: home is what you make it, and even I made a home for myself out on the prairies," he said. "But a house is more than walls too, and don't pay attention to anyone who tells you otherwise."

Luna noticed her dad shift his weight again.

"A house has memories, and not just in the timber, but the land that surrounds it," said Gordon. "You may not be tied to any one place Luna, and a bit of me is jealous of that. But I'm bound here, and it's to the bones."

"But it's just a building," Luna said, before Big Bear cut her off.

"Luna. Outside."

"What?"

"*Now*."

Gordon got up from the table. "Well, I'm feeling tired. I'll just put the dishes away, shall I? Might turn in after that."

"Thanks, Gordon," Big Bear muttered as he put his hand on Luna's back. She knew he was trying to make her move somewhere without being obvious about it, and she threw her weight against her father. He rocked back on his heels for a second before he quietly, but firmly, gripped her shoulder and began guiding her towards the door.

I'll go. But not easily, Luna thought. She wrenched herself out of his grip, then grabbed her backpack and took it with her.

They walked outside of the house to a corner of the yard that backed the edge of a sliver of woods. It was well and truly night, a soft darkness further muted by an overcast sky all quilted in clouds. As soon as they faced each other, as if by unspoken agreement, daughter and father began yelling.

"What's your problem?" they said at once.

"What's *your* problem?" Luna repeated, quickly. "You and mom *did* tell me that!"

"I also told you to read a room!" Big Bear said. Luna could tell he was angry, but she felt something else there too—sadness maybe, and, over everything else, disappointment in how his daughter had behaved. That last one hurt most of all.

"How dare you tell that old man his house means nothing when coming back to it *clearly* meant so much to him? It's the mill all over again. I don't get it—you say you don't like people telling you where to go, then you go and tell them *where to go*," he said.

"Oh, whatever," Luna said. "I'm not telling Gordon where to go. I'm just saying he doesn't have to stay here. Besides: 'Home can be anywhere, home is what you make it,'" her voice took on a mocking sing-song tone. "That was like, your and mom's motto."

"And we believed in it! Not only that—we lived it. We told you those words because we travelled all the time, and we were worried that sort of life would be hard on you. We didn't want you to feel different from other kids."

"*Thanks*, Dad. *Good* job."

She'd cut him. She knew because he winced. His face made Luna feel sore inside—but her fire was up, and she had to let it burn itself out.

Big Bear's voice gentled. "I'm sorry, Luna. If you feel that way, I really am sorry. The reason I keep doing these trips and taking you with me is because exploring the world, seeing it top to bottom . . . that was always important to me and mom. She always said the world is the best school you can attend, and I agree. The more you travel, the more you learn, and the more you . . . it's hard to explain. The more you start seeing which woods you should go into, and which ones you shouldn't."

"I can't learn that if I don't ever go in the woods, Dad," Luna said.

To her surprise, Big Bear nodded. "I know," he said, and something about the tone of his voice suggested he really *did*. "That's the thing," he went on. "Learning by exploring is nine parts learning by mistake. But if something happened—I just. I don't want you to get hurt. You're all I have, Luna. But I also want you to learn. I'm trying to keep it all in balance."

Luna knew this was reasonable. That didn't mean it was enough.

"OK, you don't want me to get hurt," she said. "But don't pretend all our trips have me 'learning from the world' when really, I'm being treated more like a baby than kids I know who have never left the country! Did you know the Stevenson sisters are allowed to ride city buses by *themselves*? That Erica Timmons has been riding her bike twenty minutes to school on her own since she was *eight*? That Shyla Greene flew on a *plane* to see her grandma without her parents? While I am going here, there, and everywhere, but always with you looking over my shoulder!"

Big Bear looked somewhere between angry and miserable. "I . . . I get that. And I get that this is hard for you. But I can't change how I feel . . . "

"What about 'home can be anywhere?' You sure seem to have changed how you feel about that." Luna snapped.

"That's not fair," Big Bear said. "Those words—they're true. But they're also a . . . "

"A *lie*?"

"No! A . . . story. A story isn't a lie. It can be different things to different people. There wasn't really a Red Riding Hood, and she didn't really meet a wolf in the woods, but you *do* have to be careful around strangers."

"In the original story, the wolf eats Red Riding Hood," Luna said.

"*That's why I want you to be careful when you go off on your own!*" Big Bear took a deep breath. "The point is, 'home being anywhere' is real, in a story way. For mom and I it was a way of getting you to believe in this life we lead, where we're not rooted in any one place. We needed you to believe in us."

"So, a lie." Luna couldn't believe what she was hearing—the words that had kept her and her father happy on the road were basically a commercial for his way of life.

An edge crept back into her dad's voice. "Mom and I *did* believe home can be anywhere. That can be the road, and that can be a place where your family has lived for generations. And the reason we are out here right now is because that means, for Gordon, it can absolutely be this house! You need to respect that. We're his guests. We need to act like it."

Luna rolled her eyes. "I wasn't trying to be mean to Gordon. I really think he'd be happier if his happiness wasn't so tied up in this house."

Big Bear scoffed. "Listen to yourself! For someone

who doesn't like being told what to do, you're sure OK with telling people what to do. He's *from* here."

"Well I *know* this place too, Dad. Especially the woods," she said and reached into her backpack and took out the pinecone—her very own piece of the Heart of the Forest. When she lifted the pinecone up, she felt power arise inside of her, power that grew out of the special grove where she had faced a monster by herself and won her quest.

Her feeling of triumph was interrupted though, because a sound was coming from far in the trees behind Big Bear. If it came from the air or the ground, or both at once, Luna couldn't tell. It had a wispy quality, like an amplified murmur broadcast by hidden microphones. Whatever the noise was, her dad hadn't heard it. He was pacing like a dog in a kennel. "Oh, sorry Luna—you *know* these woods. God, you are a smart kid, you really are, but can you balance that big brain with just a *drop* of humility?"

But Luna wasn't paying attention to her dad's words. She was watching the forest come alive behind him.

The cloud murk she walked into a few days ago, out by the cliffs, was creepy, but its creepiness arose out of its mystery. It had been impossible to see what was inside of it. The fog threading through the trees behind her dad right this minute wasn't as thick as what she'd seen on the cliffs, but it was far more terrifying because Luna could make out the shapes within. And those shapes had crawled out of her nightmares.

Here: a corpse, bloated and pale, his eyes dripping seawater. Kelp dangled from his waist and dragged on the forest floor. There: a young woman in a long nightgown, clutching her bleeding hands together, her eyes replaced by two patches of pale fire. Behind her came a short man with an auburn beard, dark leggings, a huge knife at his belt, a cap stained wet and rust red, and ember eyes that reminded her of Billy.

All of these figures were blurry, like they had been smeared with a giant thumb. But the thing that made Luna's legs turn to water was a woman whose features were distinct and defined. She moved with the haughty indifference of a queen. Not that she was dressed like one. Far from it: she wore a dress spotted with dirt, and her dark hair streamed behind her ragged and unkempt, as if it blew in a never-ending gale.

Luna weaved a kenning for her: *Gale Hair*.

It wasn't just her appearance that unsteadied Luna. It was her intent, the way she zeroed in on Big Bear and walked—no, *floated*, because her legs did not touch the ground—straight towards him, flexing fingers bent like fishhooks that ended in nails sharp as a gutting knife. Her dad had his back to the forest and was completely oblivious to the spirits and the noise they made, like the tearing of an enormous piece of construction paper.

Luna looked on in horror as more apparitions shimmered into being. She waved her arms at them, which made Big Bear raise an eyebrow. But the ghosts did not shrink away. Instead, they came on brighter, shining with more clarity, and in the case of Gale Hair, more purpose.

"Stop!" Luna yelled.

Big Bear huffed. "No, Luna, I won't stop. I've told you this time and again—*home* matters to people. *Home* is what people build their lives around. And I can't have you questioning someone on their home *in* their home—"

And then, Gale Hair glided towards Big Bear, silent as a shark, and just as he said *home* for a fourth time, she touched his neck with her taloned hands. Luna watched as her father went pale as, well, a ghost. His brown skin blanched to a sickly lemon yellow. His brown eyes frosted into the grey of a winter sky. His limbs went stiff, and then they went slack, and Big Bear reached a hand towards his daughter before he fell forward, silently, onto the grass.

7

Time froze. More spirits emerged from the trees, flowing around Luna and Big Bear like water around a rock. Luna, who had wanted to see ghosts her whole life, completely ignored them as they passed her. She only had eyes for her father, laying stiff and still on the grass.

Luna heard her own voice from far away, like it was whispering from the other side of the yard.

"Dad," she said. Then, louder, "*Dad.*"

Had he moved? Maybe the slightest shift of weight, but that could have been his body settling onto the soft ground, or the wind whispering over his hair.

Then something *did* move. But it was inside of him.

Thin lines of bluish white light seeped from Big Bear's hands, feet, and head. They pulsed, bright and dim and bright again, and Luna swore she heard music, a soft singing at the very edge of her hearing. The strings of energy that came out of her father all flowed into a single point, between his chest and throat, where they threaded together into a ragged, glowing blue ball.

"*Bear*," Luna shouted, reaching for the ball of light, unsure why, except something inside her screamed that the light was as important as his beating heart—

But is it still beating, she thought. *What if it stopped bea . . . Don't think that, don't think that.*

—she had to touch the light, grab it, force it—somehow—back into his body, his stopped body, which made no sense because he was a wanderer, someone who *moved*, except now he was not moving; he was still, too still, but still, she could seize the *light*.

Until something else did.

Gale Hair floated nearby. She drifted over the grass, then hovered over Big Bear, tall, terrible, triumphant. Her hair spilled into the sky like an oil slick; her eyes, alive— *the only thing about her that is alive*, Luna thought—with intense craving, even longing.

The ghost bent over, and her lanky fingers stretched even longer. The hint of a smirk tugged on her lips, which were caked with something white: maybe frost, maybe salt, maybe both. She unfolded her fishhook hands and scooped up Big Bear's ball of light, which immediately began fading. Luna thought she heard the faintest moan escape her father's lips, before Gale Hair cupped the blue glow in her hands and grinned, revealing a mouth of long, yellow teeth.

Luna screamed. If Gale Hair heard her, she did not care. Instead, she made a noise that fell somewhere between a contented sigh and a cat's purr. Her eyes flashed, once, with the same blue light that emerged from Big Bear. Then she floated away, moving into the night, with the light of Luna's father still clutched in her claws.

Luna stood there, frozen. She, who had fought a battle of wits with Billy and walked through the sick smoke woods by herself, stood there, helpless.

Now the cold shock was melting away, like snow in the sun. Luna began running in the direction the ghost had gone, her heart heaving, her lungs raw, yelling "Stop. Stop!"

But Gale Hair was gone. She had left no trace of her passing; not even the grass was trampled, because she had never set foot on it. Instead, there was cold air and empty space and—

—Big Bear.

"Dad," Luna said, kneeling by his side. "Oh God, Dad." She felt the cold damp of the ground soak through her knees and cursed. "Dad. *Dad*. Please, wake up."

His eyes were closed.

Luna reached out, hesitantly. Usually, her chestnut skin was light against his copper complexion; now it looked twice as dark and felt ten times warmer. Trembling, shuddering, Luna pushed her dad's eyes open—then gasped. There was no fire behind his eyes. No wit, or warmth, or even anger—and she would have traded the world for his anger, for any sign of Big Bear. But he was utterly silent, and cold.

"*Dad, speak to me! Don't be gone!*"

"Well, he's not dead."

"Dad?"

"*Dead*. But he's not."

Luna whipped her head around. It had sounded like the person was speaking right by her ear.

But then a man stepped out of the forest. Except he did not step, because he had no feet. He barely had any solidity at all; he was blue-white and faded, like a photograph left in the sun for too long. He was tall and thin, with an angular face framed by messy hair and a long moustache. He wore an old, scratchy shirt and carried a wooden shield all nicked with dents and scars. A rust-eaten axe hung from his belt. His hair would have looked yellow in the daylight, but Luna knew this person—this ghost—had not seen daylight, or any light, in a long time.

A gust of cold air passed, and the man rippled like paper in a breeze. He began to advance. Icicles of fear lanced into Luna's heart, and instinct rushed into her limbs. She grabbed the pinecone from the Heart of the Forest and held it in front of her.

The ghost stopped and held a hand in front of his face, like he was protecting his eyes from the sun. "Please. No," he said, in a voice brittle as dry grass. "I won't hurt you. I wouldn't have hurt you when I lived, and I was a warrior then. But now I am only this. A shadow. I'll leave you alone if you want, but I swear by the One-Eyed One. I just want to look at that poor fellow." He gestured to Big Bear.

Luna was a barely knit together jumble of grief, fear, and confusion, but the steel trap of her mind remembered its mythology. "You swore on 'the One-Eyed One,'" she said. "You mean Odin?"

It was strange to see relief pass over someone's face when that face was made of mist. "I passed from life so long ago the world has become unrecognizable," said the man. "And yet, to hear it from your mouth, the old gods are still worshipped by our descendants. I am glad to hear it."

Luna wasn't sure how to respond, but she *was* pretty sure this ghost—this *Viking*, it seemed—was not a threat. He looked lost, and sadness seemed to drip off him, but she didn't detect any aggression.

Yet.

The ghost moved forward again, but slower, still wary of the pinecone. Luna wasn't sure what power the cone had over ghosts. *Why didn't I use it against Gale Hair?* she thought, angrily. But now she knew some spirits reacted to it the way she reacted to spirits: with caution, even fear. She filed the knowledge away in her brain for safekeeping.

The spirit floated in front of her. "You can call me Trygve," he said. "That means 'trustworthy' in your tongue."

"We'll see. I'm Luna. You said my dad wasn't . . . You told me . . . " She paused, collected herself. "How do you know my dad isn't . . . *dead*?" She had to force herself to say it.

Trygve's eyes mushed into the rest of his face, and Luna realized he was squinting. He looked at Big Bear like her dad was a painting in a museum.

"His essence remains. Or rather, it *exists*. Just not here," the Viking said.

Luna gave him a questioning look.

"Every being has an essence," the ghost went on. "A ghost is only essence. You have essence and form. I have essence and no form. But *he* is only form. Only a body. His essence has been stolen away."

"Then he *is* dead," Luna said, choking back a sob.

"No," said Trygve. "Like I said: his essence remains. It is just not inside of him. He is hollow. Essence would still cling to him if he were dead—it lingers, you know—but his is wrenched out. He is a doll with no straw."

Luna rocked back on her heels, remembering the blue ball of light, and the way Gale Hair scooped it up.

"The . . . the ghost with the long hair. It took him," she said.

The Viking's brow lost cohesion for a moment, and strange as the moment was, Luna was oddly satisfied that she could see, through his shifting features, that he was confused. She was learning the shape of ghosts, and the more she learned them, the faster she could fight them.

"Long hair?" Trygve asked.

"A woman," Luna said. "Tall. Wild hair. Wild eyes. And long fingers . . . claws? I'm not sure." She shivered at the memory.

Trygve shuddered as well, his fog-like outline blurring and contracting; it looked like he was about to dissolve. "I know that spirit," he said. "I am older than she, but she strikes fear in me like I strike fear in the living. She is a terror."

Luna frowned. "Are you saying she's like a ghost for ghosts?"

Trygve nodded. "That one is not to be underestimated. I do not know why, but it is as if she draws her strength from the land itself."

Luna's stomach curdled like sour milk. "Then how can I save my dad? I don't understand. Why are their ghosts for *ghosts*? Why are there even ghosts here?"

"I do not know, and I am a ghost," Trygve said. "But I can guess. In the ocean, there are fish the size of my little finger, and some the size of my arm, and whales the length of ten men laid head to toe. Some larger still. The world hungers for diversity of shape and size and power in the living, so it should not surprise us that it is the same for the dead. Now: as to why the dead walk here? Well, we always have."

"But why haven't I seen any of you?" Luna asked. "I've been here for days! I haven't seen a ghost." *Just a magic forest*, she thought.

Trygve shook his head. "Rest assured, ghosts have seen you. We whisper in tree hollows and call your name in the dry wind. We are always there, if invisible to mortal eyes."

"Well, you're pretty visible now."

"That," Trygve said, with a small sigh that seemed to briefly, literally, deflate him, "is true. I just told you spirits are always around you. Until now, to be a ghost is to be half present. We can see the world, and sometimes people see us. We are aware there are other spirits. We . . . show up, and observe, and, sometimes, call out. And that is all that compels us. But not now. Things have changed. *Something* has snapped. You want to help your father, yes?"

"Of course."

"I never wanted to *do* anything as a ghost. But ever since that *something* broke, I have felt more *present*, and I want . . . well, I *want*."

"Want what?" Luna's curiosity was impossible to suppress, even with her father lying on the grass a few feet away from her.

"I am not sure. I think being a ghost is being unable to move on. So . . . I would like to move on? To whatever is . . . *supposed* to happen when we expire? Not that I can be sure of what that is."

Based on the ghost stories she had read, this made sense to Luna. "So that means you probably need to finish something in this world. Or fix something."

The Viking's face wisped again; it looked like fog curling around a dock at dawn. Luna wondered if this was the face Trygve put on when he was avoiding a question, and decided not to press it, because other questions needed answering.

"Well, whatever you want to do, this is what I *need* to figure out: my dad is out there right now, or, I don't know, his essence is. You said something snapped—maybe I can unsnap it?"

The ghost shrugged, causing his arms to rip apart, briefly. "When I lived, I saw Thor split a great-grandfather of a tree that stood by my home place. A lightning bolt ripped the trunk as a knife cuts through butter. It cut a wound into the world. You could *smell* it. Whatever 'snapped' was like that: a hole cut across water and air and stone and soil. Something opened, and through the opening the dead streamed through. And it seems that tide of the dead took something from you."

"The tide of dead people didn't do it. It was one ghost. And she didn't take some*thing*," Luna said. Hot tears burned her eyes. "It was some*one*. And I aim to get him back."

She turned then, feeling like time was already running out for her to follow Gale Hair and her father, or whatever part of her father had been stolen away. But—wait. Even if she didn't know how to fix this problem, the Viking had helped give her a better idea of what it was. So, she quickly turned back, said, "Thank you," and held her hand out.

The Viking nodded but when he reached for Luna's hand, his own plunged through Luna's palm and she saw—and *felt*—it run straight into her elbow.

A blizzard roared into Luna's chest. Ice gripped her heart. She screamed and swung the pinecone in front of her. Immediately, the ghost winced and pulled his hand away, and as he did, the chill withdrew. But Luna still felt a part of it inside her, lingering, a kernel of frost that refused to melt.

The Viking looked miserable. "I swear to you, I did not know that would happen." His face cycled through several expressions, all dark: pain, confusion, and exhaustion.

"I'm sorry everything is strange, Trygve, I really am. But my dad needs me," she said, quickly, turning again to leave.

But Trygve floated forward in front of her.

"You are going on a quest," he said. "That's as plain as the fire in your hair. What isn't plain is: where has your father gone? Where has that ghost taken him? And most importantly," Trygve added, and Luna thought she heard the barest hint of hope in his voice, "do you need a scout to help you find them?"

8

A *quest*, Luna thought. *An adventure. Like I always wanted.*

Except it wasn't. This time she had not wandered around until she found danger. Indeed, this time, the danger ignored her.

But then it took my dad, she thought. *Maybe he was right. Maybe I'm not ready to set off on my own. Maybe if I do, I'll hurt myself. Except I'm not hurt. I'm standing here thinking about what to do, and my father* . . .

Her face loosened as grief wrapped around her heart. She tried to ignore it and focus on what the Viking had just said.

"What do you mean, a *scout*?" Luna asked.

"That was my role in life," Trygve went on. "Not to

hold the shield wall, but to be a scout: the eyes that led the spear and the sword."

"I know what a scout is. What I meant was . . . you can scout . . . for me?"

Trygve nodded. Luna felt a small spark kindle in her heart.

"So your job," Luna asked, "was to find things?"

Trygve nodded. "The *skalds*—the battle poets—sang of me. Said I moved fast as *huginn* . . . "

Luna remembered what Big Bear had told her on the cliffs those days ago.

"*Huginn* means thought," she said.

Trygve nodded. "You would make a fine scout, for you not only notice things, but place them in their right order in your mind. The mind is as dangerous as the sharpest sword. In any case, yes: *huginn* is thought, and nothing is fast as thought. Everyone praised Trygve the quick . . . "

Let's be quick, then, Luna thought. "Very nice," she said. "Can you help me find my dad?"

The Viking grunted and pointed north. "I think the thing that took your father flies this way. There's a trail she leaves—not footprints, more like . . . an impression. Of misery and anger and other such feelings. I can follow it."

Trygve began walking, and Luna moved to follow, but first she looked at her father, lying in the grass. Something was off about him—and not just the fact his soul had been ripped from his body. Where before he looked pale, now he seemed to glow with soft radiance.

"What's happening to him?"

The ghost's eyes darkened. "I believe his body . . . is fading. The flesh is tied to its essence, but now the essence is gone. His form will follow his spirit, which is to say, his body will eventually be with that . . . thing that took him."

Luna's breath caught, and her cheeks grew hot with sadness and rage. "I'm not letting that happen," she said. She leaned in front of her dad and whispered to his silent, shimmering face, "I will be back. I promise. And I'll make you better."

Then she turned quickly. Trygve nodded, and said, in a low, cold voice: "Follow me."

He led her through the streets of Gordon's neighbourhood. The Viking moved silently, while Luna made long strides to match his strange, ghostly gait.

Luna was desperate to see any hint of her dad. As she kept scanning the horizon for a sign of him, her eyes took in Dove Cove at night. Streetlights shone on the wet ground, reflecting the asphalt into the sky. Luna had wandered around here at this hour before, and there had always been noise: music on the radio, or murmured conversations, or a hockey game on TV. Now everything was wrapped in inky black that rubbed the edges off sound. A kenning birthed itself in Luna's mind: *death quiet*.

But if it was quiet, it was not *still*. Shapes and impressions moved in the dark, outlines of beings who had woken up after a long sleep. It was as if the night had lifted a curtain on the world's ghosts, even as it concealed the sights and sounds of the living. There must have been dozens of them, but they were distant, barely visible—to Luna, they looked like the shimmer in the air on an exceptionally hot day.

But the ghost she both feared and wanted to see more than any, the one who had her father, was now nowhere to be seen.

Every now and then a shape slipped from the shadows and moved towards Luna. But, remembering how Trygve had reacted to the pinecone, she would hold it in front of her. The shapes would hesitate, then retreat into the dark.

"That cone," Trygve asked. "How did you come by it?"

"I found it," Luna said, very quickly.

"Where?"

"... In the woods."

Not technically a lie, she thought. *Just not the whole truth.*

She wasn't sure why she didn't tell Trygve where her shard of the Heart of the Forest came from, except she knew it carried power and Trygve recognized that. She was willing to use this Viking to find her father, but despite his name, she did not fully trust him.

"Why are you so interested in it?" Luna asked. She was walking faster now, and her lungs were beginning to burn from the effort. It was strange to see a ghost give her a skeptical glance out of the side of his eyes, but Trygve did just that.

"Because the power in that thing is obvious to anything with spirit's sight," he said. "It is a light that draws those of us from the other side like a flame calls a moth. That seed cup"—*he made a kenning, Luna thought*—"has great magic, wherever it may be from." Trygve gave her another sidelong look. "But a good scout knows when information is not easily forthcoming. So, I will leave it at that. For now."

"Good," Luna said.

Trygve grunted. "See how the wind blows the small ghosts around? It wants to move me as well. But these are weak spirits, without will. Do you know what it's like to wander past death's fence with no direction? Finding your father is a mission, a direction. And like I said before, I have lacked direction for . . . well, I don't know for how long. You have given me a task, and thus I won't blow away so easily." He paused and looked around. "We need to change course. Just a little. Walk this way."

The Viking pointed in a direction totally devoid of light.

Luna's throat tightened. "How do you know they went that way?" she asked.

"Because that is where it is darkest."

Soon Dove Cove petered away into long fields of rain-splattered grass. Luna could only see a few feet in any direction. And she would not have even seen that small distance were it not for the pale ghost-light that emanated off Trygve.

And then—Trygve and Luna were at the ocean.

The ground under their feet had grown colder, harder. All trace of the town was gone, replaced by an endless beach. There were stones, everywhere: little pebbles bleached white in the sun, and big boulders that looked like sleeping trolls. The waves curled and shook the land when they slapped it.

Luna stood on the lonely shore.

A sliver of moon peaked out from the murky clouds, accompanied by a few lost stars. But the little light only emphasized how vast the land was, and how small she was in comparison to it.

This wasn't the adventure she had dreamt of. Fighting Billy had been dangerous, but in a way, simple. This felt . . . complicated. And *heavy*. Her mind took in the darkness, and the questions that rushed in with it.

Can I trust a ghost named "Trustworthy?" How do I get Bear away from Gale Hair? What happened when I broke the pinecone off the tree?

And finally, the question she wanted to push furthest away: *Is this my fault?*

She looked at the Viking, and saw, in his ghost eyes, some kind of understanding. But whatever he understood, they didn't have time to discuss it.

"What do we do now?" Luna asked.

In reply, the scout scanned the horizon: the cold, black night; the whispering ocean; and, in the distance, the shapes that moved where those things met. Sharply, Trygve whispered into the night. "Luna. Look to the water."

At first, she saw nothing. The sky came down to the sea like a curtain on a stage, concealing the world behind it. But if the ocean absorbed the moonlight, it held it as well, and in its reflection, Luna saw a shadow: loping, scrabbling, striding over the waves like they were hills, away from the shore and further onto the ocean. The shadow was dark, even against the black water, but it had form: that of a tall, spidery body, lit underneath by the moonlight and the foam, and topped with hair that flowed wildly in a never-ending breeze. In the spider shadow's hands was a blue glow.

"It crosses the waves," Trygve said.

"Then we follow it!" Luna shouted. "Hurry up!" Her mind emptied itself of fear and self-doubt and bent in its entirety towards following her father. She rushed from the beach into the water—and gasped. When the first wave struck her, it felt as cold as Trygve's touch.

Luna had swum in cold water before. She would not let the elements deter her. She jumped into the sea without hesitation, the icy wet flowing over her hair, her hoodie, and her back. She kept her hand tight on the pinecone, and for some reason, it warmed her body.

But if the pinecone helped Luna withstand the cold, it did not weaken the waves. She had learned to body surf with Big Bear, who taught her to dive into each wave head-on like a torpedo. But now the swells came in rapid succession, too fast for her to dive through all of them, and one caught her full in the chest with the brute force of a bull.

What am I doing, Luna thought, as she fell backwards into the sea. *I don't know where they are going, and I can't swim to match Gale Hair's speed.*

The water flowed over her face, up her nose, and into her brain. For a moment she thought she'd never be able to breathe again. She summoned the strength of every muscle in her body and was able to pull her head out of the water, only to be smacked by the next oncoming wave. This time it rushed in her ears, seemed to gurgle, *stay, stay, never leave*, and her eyes flashed open and saw only dark water, dark night, and above that, two shapes flying in a tight circle: birds, blacker than the water and the sky.

9

Whatever Luna was sleeping on was big, and warm, and *alive*. Its heart thudded beneath her like soft thunder.

But huge as it was, it was just a speck beneath the sky that flooded Luna's vision when she opened her eyes. A sky so big she could see the curve of the Earth, so clear she could see the horizon descend around her like she was in a planetarium. For a moment, she smiled.

Then she sat up and gasped, "Where am I?"

"I will admit, I sailed many seas in my living days, but never in this fashion," said a voice at her side. Trygve was glowing softly, stroking his beard, or trying to; his fingers only passed through his chin.

They were both sitting on something smooth and wet. Slick, rubbery, almost oily. The strange surface stretched backwards and forwards the length of a school bus. All around it were waves, dark grey or almost purple, frosted with whitecaps. It was no longer night, but there was no sun in the overcast sky.

Another voice spoke up from somewhere unseen. It was a strange kind of speaking, soft and hollow, like the echoes of speech rather than speech itself. It was also *immense*, which was not the same thing as loud. If you heard the voice in a sleeping baby's room you would think it occupied every square inch of space, yet it would never wake the infant.

The ponderous voice spoke directly into Luna's head.

I am glad you're awake, it said.

"I'm glad too," she said back.

She looked at Trygve, who had a bemused smile on his face.

"Who is it?" Luna asked, half to Trygve, half to everything around her, which was where the voice was coming from.

Hello, it said. Luna gawked, as a giant fluked tail emerged from the water and slapped the surface. Spray rose in a fine silver mist, sparkling in the icy air, like the stars had come down to eye level.

"We're riding a whale?!" Luna said.

"Yes. Truly, we are on the whale roads," said Trygve.

Hello, the voice said again.

Luna saw a blowhole in front of her, surrounded by grey skin that was paler closer to the animal's head—

although she could not see its head, as it was underwater. Smooth, slick skin also stretched behind her, which likewise vanished under the sea. To her side was Trygve, her backpack, and—she realized with a quick intake of breath—the pinecone from the Heart of the Forest.

She felt a deep urge just then to hold the cone, and when she reached over and picked it up, warmth flooded into her body. The heat steadied her, which she needed. Partly because it was freezing on the whale's back; partly because she had woken up on the back of a whale that was able to speak to her through her mind.

Luna looked at Trygve. The ghost's neck fluttered, and she realized he was clearing his throat. "I saw you swim after your father," he said. "You didn't hesitate, little *bearskin*. I apologize, that word might be unfamiliar to you. It is our kenning for a warrior who is so brave they look death in the eye, then laugh."

Bearskin chasing Big Bear, Luna thought.

"As I say, you were almost mad with your bravery," Trygve went on. "And, it must be said, not a very good swimmer. The waves took you under quickly. I was sure you would drown."

"So, you summoned a whale for me? Using Viking magic?" Luna asked.

Trygve shook his head. "I am no wonder worker. *Seidr* magic is women's stuff." Luna rolled her eyes, but the Viking ignored her. "No, I thought to plunge into the water to fetch you out, but I knew my hands would only pass through you. I was not sure what to do, and worried that when I saw you next, we would be fellow spirits. But instead, the water began to roil and boil, and a great shape parted the waves, and then—the whale arose. With you on its back."

"Why?" Luna asked,

"Ask the whale. She is quite talkative."

The soft song rung in between Luna's ears again, from one side of her mind to the next.

And its message was gentle, if insistent: *You hold something special, and the weight of that power drew me to you. But before I go on about why I am here, maybe you can answer the same question for me.*

"What do you mean?" asked Luna.

I saved you because I suspect you have set many things in motion. And while being still is not one of your strengths, I suspect you are the one who can bring stillness to the land again.

Luna pondered the meaning of this, then remembered her manners. "Well, thanks. Y'know. For carrying me. Wherever we're going."

You don't weigh much. Although the weight of a thing is more than its body.

"What does that mean?" Luna asked.

Our choices have weight, too, the whale said. Luna noticed Trygve's form shift a little.

So, tell me about your choices—Why are you here? What brought you to these shores? What is it you seek?

"Which 'here'? Newfoundland? Your back?"

The whale said, *Yes*.

"Well . . . " Luna began, "I came here with my dad. And I started exploring, which is a thing I like to do. And then these ghosts came out of nowhere and one of them took my dad's . . . essence? Soul? I'm not sure. But I'm trying to get it back." She had left out an important part of the story, but it was a part she didn't feel like recalling, just yet. Instead, Luna sighed and said, "This has all been very strange."

The whale's voice rang gently between her ears. *You chased a ghost that held your father's soul only to half drown, then woke up next to a dead Viking on the back of a whale. 'Strange' is a relative term.*

"This is a clever whale," Trygve said.

Thank you, said the voice. *What of you, Northman? What brings you here?*

"Adventure is its own reward," the Viking said. "While I took breath, my companions and I left the shores of my home place to come to this far-off land, search out shores we never dreamt of, and soak ourselves in glory."

"It made you a ghost," Luna said.

"Perhaps. Better a ghost than a coward dying alone," he said.

Luna wondered what Trygve meant by that; after all, he said he'd come here with 'companions.' She also resisted the urge to roll her eyes when he talked about 'soaking himself in glory.' She had heard plenty of kids talk with the same sort of bluster on playgrounds. That didn't mean she disagreed with the Viking; she just didn't like that he wrapped the idea in such arrogant words.

But why are you guiding this girl? the whale asked.

Luna listened as she watched a nearby iceberg shed the snow on its surface glittering in its wake like silver dust.

"Something weakened the barrier between the living and the dead, and she was the first living being I had spoken with in countless moons," said the Viking. "I saw she needed aid, so I provided it."

So, is it in your heart for you to seek glory, or to help those in need?

"Can it not be both?" Trygve mumbled. Then he became silent. The quiet lasted a little too long, until Luna broke it.

"Trygve came here to explore. I get that," she said. "It's how I am. I want to see the world and have adventures. If I walk away from something interesting, I always wonder what would have happened if I had gone after it. My dad . . . " and she paused, overtaken at the thought of her father. Then she swallowed and said, " . . . my dad didn't always let me explore on my own, which *really* made me want to explore on my own."

So, I looked for adventure, she thought. *And I found it. And I broke some rules to do it. And I thought I was soaked in glory.*

And I took this pinecone.

She ran her finger over the bumpy *seed cup*, as Trygve called it, then looked at the ocean, dark as spilled ink. Icebergs bobbled here and there, frigid and blue. Whenever the wind blew—which was always—it scraped the ice and smeared it onto Luna's face. The cold reached into the deepest parts of her and refused to let go.

"I'm a hellraiser," she whispered. "Like my mom before me." She had wanted to believe this for a long time, and it always felt like her dad was standing in the way of it. But now she was saying it out loud, the words sounded a little small. Like kids bragging on a playground.

So, you think you're following in your mother's footsteps? asked the whale.

"A little," Luna said. "She did cool stuff. What's cooler than exploring a magic forest?"

Crossing a magic ocean? I'm not sure. Is that why you're here now?

"No," said Luna. "I'm here now because I need to help my father."

That is a good reason. Where did you find that pinecone you are holding?

Luna said nothing.

Trygve stared at her. "Now we are getting to the marrow in the bone," he said.

"I don't see what that has do with anything," she muttered.

But before she could make any more excuses to avoid the question, the world provided her with one. Luna's focus shifted to the horizon, and her eyes widened. She had been noticing how everything on the ocean felt small compared to the immensity of the water, even the icebergs. But what she had just spotted was growing larger with each passing second.

Trygve was watching Luna, not the ocean. "Do you see your father?" he asked.

"I ... I don't think so. No. That's definitely not him."

"What do you mean ... " Trygve began to say, but then he was staring too.

The shape on the horizon was growing, closer and in size: a boat, haunted and dark, sailing directly towards them.

10

Fear prickled Luna's neck as the boat approached. Kelp and seaweed waved from the rigging like a drowned man's hair. The sails were torn, with holes from clew to luff, although they somehow still billowed in the wind. The planks were black and shone with wet decay.

Luna made a kenning: the *rotship*.

The day was dark, the dead boat far away. But the craft skipped over the waves like an evil stone, heading in their direction true as an arrow. As it drew closer, Luna could make out the rotship's crew, a scrabbling crowd of inky shapes, jostling against each other.

A wet corpse with eyes of blue fire. A man with lank seaweed hair, skin the colour of algae, and webbed hands that ended in claws. A monster with a tentacled beard and the lure of an anglerfish dangling off their shrouded head. A bearded warrior with barnacle-encrusted skin, holding a long-hafted rusted axe in a hand that resembled a lobster's claw. It did not have another hand, for its other arm ended in a wickedly sharp coral spike.

"What are they?" Luna asked.

The end of our journey, I would guess. The whale turned and swam, trying to outrun the rotship, but the craft was quickly gaining on them. *That boat moves on an ill wind, and there is no way I can outpace it.*

"Can you swim faster?" Trygve asked, his voice cracking, his body growing wispier, betraying, Luna realized, his fear. *But there's more,* she thought: the rotship was awful, but her companion seemed familiar with the terror that sailed on that boat.

Luna shouted, "Trygve—do you recognize them?"

He snapped his head around, and the rapid movement seemed to rip more of his body away. His face reformed into a frown.

"They are . . . my companions," he said. "I am sure of it. And they cannot be reasoned with."

"*Those* are your companions?" Luna asked.

"*Were* my companions," he said, frowning. "Now they are *aptrganga*."

"Apartment-gongers?"

"*Ap-tur-gonng-gah*. Again Walkers. The risen dead. With a boat, it would seem. We do not want to be caught by them."

"We might not have a choice," Luna said, as the space between the whale and the rotship rapidly shrank. "What do they want? If you recognize them, do you think they'll recognize you?"

"That is what I am worried about," Trygve said softly, almost to himself. Then louder, "They want to kill, Luna. Killing is what they did when they lived. I suppose they loved it so much they decided to keep at it in death."

Before Luna could respond, a whistle cut through the air, high and keen. It was the wind. It screamed over the waves and into Luna's face, cold as the heart of an iceberg, sharp as a knife, the sort of North Atlantic squall that sent a dozen ships to the ocean floor, except now it had been summoned to push a sunken ship across the waves.

The salty air made Luna's eyes mist over with tears, but she could still see, and floating beyond the rotship, her feet rising and falling as they barely skimmed the waves, was Gale Hair. She was moving her thin claws in the air, tracing intricate patterns. Whenever she paused, another gust roared to life. True to her name, Gale Hair was drawing the wind into existence, then launching it over the ocean, where it blew the rotship towards the whale and froze Luna's eyelashes to her face.

Luna looked desperately at Trygve, who could barely retain his shape. He was screaming to the whale: "Swim! Faster! We need to go."

"No," Luna yelled, though she knew it wasn't really her decision. "The thing that took my dad is there," she shouted, pointing at Gale Hair, even as the wind swallowed her words.

Then the rotship was practically upon them.

"You can't leave," croaked a voice. The croaker, with skin of grey mottled scales, a face draped with red kelp dreadlocks, and a fat throat sac, wet and white as a dead fish, was calling from the rail of the rotship, pointing at Luna and grinning, or grinning as much as a frog face could. Behind him, the rest of the crew waved axes and swords and looked hungrily across the narrow gap of water that separated themselves from the whale.

Trygve put his hand on his axe. He had reformed into a slightly more defined shape. *Is this the ghost version of getting a hold of yourself?* Luna wondered, although she noticed the Viking still quivered with panic.

Abruptly, Trygve's eyes swelled wide. He yelled, "Put your head down!" and Luna ducked at the exact moment a spear sailed over her head.

Now a battle cry rang out from the rotship: "Odin!"

Trygve bellowed back at them, "May the ice trolls take you, you cowards!"

Not the first insult I'd have thought of, Luna thought, but she was glad her companion had regained a measure of bravery.

Rain slashed across the sky, and the world unravelled into a panicked chaos; the Again Walkers were clamouring for blood, and the wind was howling in Luna's ears.

One creature, sporting a head that fell somewhere between a human and a red octopus, jumped from the rotship onto the back of the whale. Trygve swung at it with his axe. It tried to dodge, overbalanced, and fell backwards into the water.

Another monster, its face crusted with black limpets, drew a sword that was the nose of a sawfish. He pointed it at Luna and smiled with shark teeth that dripped with seawater.

These are not ghosts, she realized. *They are too solid, too present. Trygve said ghosts exist in a dream.*

These are nightmares.

And now a new noise entered her mind: the whale, moaning in pain. A spear quivered in its back, soaked in saltwater and blood.

Luna's voice joined the messy tangle of noise drawn over the battle. Her vision had gone as red as the whale's blood. She heard herself scream even as her mind went silent, because Luna had no use for thought now, just reflex, need, and the will to carry out her need. She did not know how it happened, only that at one point, her hands were empty, and in another moment, they held the pinecone.

The scales of the cone, white and warm, were in her wet palm, which was numb from the cold but still able to feel the cone's rises and ridges. Her arm flexed and her voice rang out again, louder, but not louder than the wind; indeed, it was as if her voice *was* the wind, and the clouds, and the sea.

Two ravens flew above her head, and she heard a voice in the deep corners of her mind: *break them with what was broken.*

By instinct, Luna held the pinecone above her head. The ocean breeze nibbled her fingers. The air was sharp and clean. The creature with the sawfish nose gave a slurping bellow and moved to jump on the whale.

Luna tightened her grip, and another wind formed, this one rolling in behind her. It flew over the ocean with a vast sucking intake, then drew the water into itself.

Luna knew, as sure as wave and stone and breath: *This is my wind. I called it into being.*

A wave arose with the air, a saltwater wall the size of a small building. Luna's wind pulled the swell closer to the whale and the rotship. Foam flecked her face like freshly driven snow.

The Again Walkers screamed once more, but now in fear and panic. Their cries were cut short by the wave smashing into their vessel.

New noises hatched: wood splintering, timbers creaking, masts snapping. The rotship reeled, tipped, and capsized. The slick bodies of the Again Walkers plopped into the cold ocean like tossed pebbles.

Luna gasped, Trygve whooped, and they both watched as the wave moved on. Much of its force had been absorbed by the rotship, but its strength was not yet spent. It rushed on, past the icebergs, to the place where Gale Hair stood on the water. Luna could not see the spirit's face, but she did see Gale Hair pause, as if reassessing the strength of this girl and the Viking who accompanied her.

Gale Hair opened her mouth. A high shriek drowned all the other sounds on the water. The noise was *sharp*; it cut through the sky, but it also felt like a hot knife cutting into Luna's brain. The noise of the ocean—the wind and the waves—cushioned the force of the scream, but not enough. Fire burned across Luna's mind; she shook her head in agony and saw Trygve clutching his chest.

There was something wet under her nose. She held her finger there for a moment and it came back, bright and red. She was bleeding.

Gale Hair stopped screaming—Luna felt her chest loosen and the pain in her head lighten immediately—and held her hand up. In her taloned fist, the glow of Big Bear's essence pulsed against the dark. Soon, the wave would sweep over both of them, drowning Big Bear's light in dark saltwater. A crooked smile cracked open Gale Hair's haggard face.

Luna yelled "No!" and made a downward slash with the pinecone, and immediately, the wave collapsed like an overturned cup of water. Its backwash made smaller waves that lapped out in every direction, but these were not sizable enough to swamp her father or the spirit who had kidnapped him.

In the distance, still holding Big Bear's essence up to the sky, Gale Hair stood on the water. She made a slight bow, followed by a mocking salute. Then she turned and continued her strange walk into the oncoming night, and the north.

11

"We have to follow them," Luna cried, but before she finished speaking, the whale moaned again. It listed to one side, enough so that Luna lost her footing on its slick skin. She landed hard on her behind and threw one hand out to steady herself.

Trygve was already standing by the spear embedded in the whale's back. He reached out to it, and while his hands had passed through Luna before, they were able to close around the spear now.

"Are you ready, great swimmer?" he asked.

The whale groaned.

Trygve did not wait for more of an answer: with a great heft, he yanked the spear out of the whale's back. More blood ran from the wound, but Luna could see the spear had not gone too deep. The whale was hurt, but the injury was not fatal.

The whale righted itself, the girl and the Viking holding on until they found stable footing in the area behind the blowhole. Then it surged forward, its moaning replaced by a bellow, a challenge to the open sea. Before, it had been laid back, almost lazy. Now it swam like a hunter.

As they moved away from the watery battlefield, Luna saw some of the Again Walkers bobbing in the water. There were less of them now, maybe five remaining. *I sent the rest to the bottom of the ocean*, she thought. The feeling became a pit in her stomach and a swell in her heart all at once.

The Again Walkers clung to the overturned hull of the rotship and watched the whale pass with venom in their eyes. They called out, in voices as scratchy as a jellyfish sting and slimy as squid ink: "Go on, Trygve. Go, like you did before. We won't be far behind. We'll find you, this time. You'll only fly so far."

The whale did not stop moving, and soon the Again Walker voices faded.

Now that the battle was over, Luna's mind was asking questions again. *Where did Gale Hair take Dad? How can we follow him? And why were those things trying to stop us?*

When the only sound was the wind—a real wind, not the bitter one summoned by Gale Hair or the tempest of Luna's storm—she turned to Trygve.

"What did they mean, 'we'll find you *this time*?' And how can they follow us?" Luna asked. "I sank their ship."

Trygve shook his head, which was growing fainter. "You cannot sink what has already been sunk."

Luna scoffed. "Uh uh. No weird, mystic answers. Tell me plainly, in words I can understand: what just happened?"

Trygve looked at her, hard. For the first time since they had met, he was angry at her. "*You* tell *me*, storm singer! I have not seen a wave like that since I crossed the sea with my companions. Where did that power come from?"

They were both raw and upset, but still, Luna had felt a thrill when Trygve called her *storm singer*. He had just wrapped her deeds into a kenning, and that made her power more real and tangible.

"I don't know, Trygve," Luna said, sensing the weight of the pinecone in her hand. "What I *do* know is those Again Walkers—they knew you. You knew them. And they weren't ghosts! They were . . . monsters. They could hold things. If I'm going to fight them, I have to know why they can throw things, or why your hand could grab that spear and yank it out of the whale, but now you're going all misty again."

As if to underline what she had just said, the wind blew Trygve's hair behind his back, where it seemed to dissolve, only to reform again a few seconds later.

The Viking crossed his arms. "You're right," he said. "The Again Walkers are *not* ghosts. That is why I named them *aptrganga*—they are dead, but different. And yes, they were my companions. I could recognize some of their faces, even through their monstrous transformation." He paused. "I once worked with those men to settle this land."

"What do you mean, settle it?" Luna asked. "No one was here before you? Did you die settling this place?"

Trygve said nothing for a long moment. Then he shook his head.

"Yes, I died settling this place. If you must know, it was quite . . . ignoble. One day I went to scout the headlands, and, like a clumsy fool, I fell into a ravine. I lay there, unable to move, in a cold misery. So, I died: not as a warrior, with a bloody axe in my hands, but helpless, and alone. It is for this shame that I have become a useless phantom."

Luna knew how to tell a story, and she knew when she was being told one. Trygve was leaving something out, just as she left something out when the whale asked her how she had come here. But she'd ignore that for now. She needed to know how to fight Again Walkers.

"It sucks that you died like that, Trygve," she said. "But that still doesn't explain why the Again Walkers are helping Gale Hair, or how they could throw a spear that hurt our friend." She patted the whale's back affectionately.

"In a way, it does," Trygve said. "See, my companions have a purpose. A simple one, but a purpose nonetheless: to fight, and kill!"

"So they attacked a whale? And me, a child?"

"A child who sings with Thor's voice! What greater challenge could there be than a storm maiden, atop a whale? Remember how the wind did not blow me in the village where we met? You gave me a mission. The more purpose a spirit has, the more solidity they gain, and in turn, the more they can touch the world. *That* is why my companions are Again Walkers, rather than mere ghosts! They are here to *fight*, and *win*. With such direction they may summon a spear that will pierce a whale! And by fighting them, we have performed a deed that the bards will sing of! Doubly so because we also faced the spirit who stole your father—the tall one with the knife scream."

Luna winced at the memory. "It's a good thing we were out on the ocean when she yelled." She shuddered to think of how strong Gale Hair's voice would have been in an enclosed space, with no outside noise surrounding it.

Trygve nodded. "In my land we spoke of the first giant, a frost-bound nightmare we called *Ymir*—the Screamer. A fitting name for that hag." The Viking frowned. "She has power. She has purpose, even if I cannot guess at it. Whereas I died with none, which is why I am just fog." He spat these last words, then paused. "Although I admit, I am not sure why I was able to hold their spear. Perhaps the dead can touch what the dead create?"

Trygve's question hung in the air for a few moments, before the thundercloud grey of the whale's back was darkened by two shadows: much smaller, and darker, and louder.

Quork. Quork.

The two ravens flapped down, onto the whale, and looked at Luna, then Trygve, then Luna again.

"Odin's thoughts . . . " said Trygve.

" . . . and memory," Luna said.

The whale's voice flooded their minds. *Your land had birds like this, Northman, but that does not mean* these *birds are* those *birds. They are part of this island. They ride its wind, just as I ride its waves. But don't take my word for it. Why don't you ask them?*

"That's silly. Birds don't talk," Luna said, but given the events of the last few days, her words didn't have much conviction.

And then came a voice—no, two voices—deep and scratchy, as rough as the scales of the pinecone Luna had used to summon the storm.

The voices said: *You say birds don't talk. But whales do?* The ravens stood on the back of the whale.

We know the Odin birds, Northman, they said. *They see and seek, like us. But the whale is right. We hatched here, nest here. Yet we fly everywhere. Know all our cousins. The black-feathered family entire. We fly through the Viking lands and the Haida lands and the Hellas lands and the Chukchi lands. We are not all the same, but related. Kin. Prophets.*

"You *can* talk?" Luna said. "I thought I heard your voices during the battle. So why didn't you say anything before? When I saw you in the forest?"

Just because we can talk doesn't mean we like to. Especially to humans. We much prefer bird words. And in the forest we did not need words for you to listen to us.

Luna made a kenning for their voices: the *croak wind*.

The birds ruffled their feathers. *We watched. Made sure you did what you needed to do, until you didn't. And by that time, you were not listening to anyone. Maybe not even yourself.*

"What do they mean?" Trygve asked.

They mean whydja whydja whydja, thought Luna, ignoring the Viking and squeezing the pinecone, remembering the screams that rang through the woods when she was alone with the Heart of the Forest.

Trygve looked at her for a moment, then turned to the birds.

"Clever ravens, I once sailed under your banner. My people said your kind witness all that occurs under the sun, can answer all questions. Did you observe my hand gain the weight and heft to fight my former companions? To lift that spear out of this whale? Why did I have that power?" Trygve asked.

Saw it, Northman, came the croak wind. *Saw your hand go strong and solid with purpose. Saw the girl pluck a storm from the sky like we pluck an eye from a corpse. Saw her find power, then hold it back. Odd choice for one who seemed so eager to find magic: once she held it, she decided not to use it.*

"You mean when I stopped the wave from hitting Gale Hair? I was trying not to hurt my dad," Luna said.

Now the whale's voice rose from the water, a soothing gong to the ravens' rough throats. *Maybe holding power back is the greater use of it. Maybe she can do more than fight monsters and lay a storm on the world; is there not room for healing it too?*

Luna nodded. "I think that's something my mom would have said, y'know? She was a soldier. She was a—"

I believe the word you used was 'hellraiser?' the whale answered.

Luna's face split into a crooked grin as she remembered words her father had said—technically just a few days ago, although it felt like a lifetime.

"Yeah. But she was more. Mom was brave. Sometimes, she broke the rules. Gaga—that's my grandma—said she just didn't like being told what to do. Like, Mom loved their neighbours, but when she was a kid, around my age, she would sneak into their barn, just to look at their tools and tractors, even though all she had to do was ask permission. And I think Mom liked to mess with people, but in a nice way. Sort of nice way."

Sort of? asked the whale.

"Like, this one time she secretly brought a frog she caught with her to sleepaway camp even though the rules said no pets. Then she put *another* frog onto the pillow of the girl who told on her." Luna laughed.

"But mainly," she went on, remembering the words of her father on the cliff in front of the forest, "she helped people in trouble. She hated it when people were *really* hurt. Even the frog thing—she told the girl sorry after, and they ended up becoming friends. Later she wanted to see the world and do something good for it. That's why, when she got older, she joined the army, even though her parents didn't like it. But she joined as a doctor. She went to dangerous places, then stuck around to make people better."

Luna fell into her memories. When her mom died in the accident, it was so *sudden*. She had cried, and the hurt had been so bad it ached, but Luna had years to figure out her pain, and not so many solid memories to pin her grief on. One of her aunts told her, "You'll always think of your mom, but you've got a lot of living to fill the space she left."

Big Bear, on the other hand . . . her dad did a good job of smiling through the sad, but it still washed over him. Sometimes every day. So yes, she missed her mom. But it wasn't just the person. It was the unit they had all been, and the lightness that had been snatched from them.

"When she left, it was like . . . like more than my mom went away. Ever since she died, dad has been so worried about me it makes him not see straight. I know why he gets worried, I do, but . . . it's *constant*. And I just want to go where I want to go." Luna sighed.

The whale's voice whispered again. *A parent might agree. But they want to see you get there safely. What must it be like to lose part of your heart? And then see it, reflected in someone so close to the person who has gone . . .* The song was gentle, but a sharp edge crept around it. *But there is more. Keep telling us your story.*

The ravens joined in. *Tell us. Tell us what you know. It is our role to hear it. Your role to tell it.*

Luna watched the water. She knew what the birds and the whale wanted to hear. It was the thing she least wanted to say. The cone was heavy in her hand, which was odd, because it felt like such a trophy just a day ago.

But a lot had changed between yesterday and today.

"Well," Luna began, "one day I went into a forest. But it was a special forest. A forest that . . . well, it was sort of like one forest but then it was *all* the forests, everywhere, all at once. Does that make sense?"

The ravens spoke up. *Like a chain. Each link is part of the whole. What happens if you break a chain link?*

"It . . . breaks the whole chain," Luna said. "Whatever it was holding gets loose. Even one link can loosen everything." She looked at the cone, white as snow.

The ravens cried out, *Loose. It is loose,* over and over, in the chattering way of birds.

The whale simply thought, *Yes*.

"Wait, you silly, giant fish and ash-cloaked birds," said Trygve. "Are you saying the seed cup the girl whips about her head held death from life? That breaking it from the first tree caused ghosts to return to the world? I thought it just gave her the power to make storms."

The ravens flapped their wings as they screamed. *The Heart holds many things. It can hold the storm. And it held death back from life.* They looked at Luna. *You hold part of the Heart, but a Heart is part of a whole. Taken from the tree, there is a hole in the whole.*

"But even though I took it from the tree, it is . . . 'working' for me, right?" Luna said. "I summoned the wind back there."

The birds hopped. *Your will and desire are strong. You unleashed a little storm, maybe because there is a storm inside of you. Storms have power and give you strength, even when you could not summon a real one. We saw that. Saw you could save the Heart from the goat-legged thing that tried to eat it.*

"Long story," Luna said, seeing Trygve's questioning face. "Another monster. It wanted to chew on the Heart, forever. Which I'm pretty sure would have poisoned and destroyed everything it was connected to." She held up the pinecone. "I got it to eat a rock instead."

"I am not sure I feel wiser," the Viking said softly.

The thing that tried to eat the Heart was desire, said the ravens. *It saw the yearning in the girl, the need to prove herself, and called to her too. The Billy thing wanted a meal.* Luna's throat tightened, as she remembered her confrontation with Billy.

The ravens' croak wind blew on. *We helped the girl find the goat legs. We thought she could save the Heart. She* did. But then, she broke it. And the illness from the breaking spread like lichen on bark. She must put the piece of the Heart back. Put death back. When the Heart is whole and there is no hole, balance will be restored. If she wants to return death to its place, she must first return life to where she robbed it from.

"What does *that* mean?" Luna asked. "*Where* does that mean? Return the pinecone to where I found it? How do I get *there*? Like, I don't know anything about forests or magic, not really."

The voice from the water sang again. *Whales only know so much about land sort of things. What is the purpose of a pinecone?*

"I guess... they're like seeds?" Luna said, remembering Trygve's kenning—*seed cup*—for the cone.

The ravens opened their beaks, fluffed their feathers, and let off a long string of rasps and croaks.

"Excuse me?" Luna asked, but the birds kept chanting a raw chorus, sounding like wind coiling in thunderheads that darkened an angry sky. She spoke again, impatiently. "Stop! Please. Even if I figure out how to take the cone, the... seed cup—gah, whatever, you know what I mean— even if I get *it* back to the Heart of the Forest..." She paused. She knew how selfish this sounded, but her curiosity and desire pushed her to ask it, "... will I lose the power it gives me?"

Quiet fell. Neither birds nor whale said anything. Luna wondered if that silence was its own answer.

Sunlight shattered on the water like an upturned jar of stars, but Luna's thoughts were of the thundercrack and tidal wave she sang into being. She had just come into this power, and, truth be told, she was a little scared of it. She had felt the strength of the storm at her beck and call, but those elements were like angry buffalo—wild, full of danger. She remembered Gale Hair, standing in the path of the wave Luna had created, holding a piece of Big Bear that seemed impossibly fragile. The possibility of her power made Luna terrified and excited all at once. She had always known she was capable of anything; now, thanks to the pinecone, she could do a Great Thing that no one else could.

As if listening to her thoughts, Trygve spoke up. "These animals are asking too much. Luna has strength, and the will to use it. She is a warrior, and you cannot ask her to give up that which makes her one."

Luna had nodded along to everything Trygve said, but now she paused.

"You . . . you're not wrong, Trygve. I *do* like this power." It was a relief to say that, to confess to how tempting the pinecone was. "But doing what I want, when I want to, doesn't make me a warrior. And neither does the seed cup, even if it lets me summon storms."

"What makes you a warrior then?" the Viking asked.

Luna looked at the place where the water and sky met. Not for the first or last time, she wondered why air fresh off the ocean tasted so good.

"You know," she said, "when I saw the tree this pinecone was attached to, it was pitiful. Some monster spent all his time scratching and poisoning it." She remembered the forest and feeling like she was a tree growing into, and out of, the land. "Billy was terrible to the tree, the Heart of the Forest. He was sucking the life out of it because he thought it would fill him up, but it didn't. But even that monster never broke the branch."

She breathed out. "But I did. And it brought the dead back. Including the thing that took my father. Which means if I can send the dead back—I can *save* him."

Wind and waves were the only sound for a very long moment.

Then the ravens took to their wings, making ever expanding circles over the whale, calling in cold, clean voices, *The story is told. A good start. You need a true beginning to reach a true end. You named the choice you made in the forest. Now you can fix what has come of it.*

Luna watched the ravens dance on the icy breeze that bore down on the ocean. After the birds shrank to specks on the sky, she glanced at Trygve. But the Viking only stared at the sea.

A rocking, a slight dip. Spray leapt up the whale's back. The soft thunder of its song filled Luna's mind. *To fix the land, you must cross the water. Your story paid that passage. But it put a burden on your heart. Why don't you trade your saltwater for mine?*

Luna sighed.

She knew how to cry. Losing her mother had been a lesson in knowing, and dealing, with grief, even at the age of five. This was a new kind of crying. She had just given her mistake a shape and size and weight, and it pressed heavy on her heart.

So Luna wept, quietly, but she did not hold anything back. Her tears ran free.

The wind blew the ocean's saltwater into her eyes, replacing her tears. Her legs got shaky.

Then something changed. The soft ripping in her heart scarred into flinty resolve—hard and sure and solid. She would make the Heart whole, draw the line between the dead and the living, send Gale Hair away, and save her father—or she would die trying.

12

Luna and the Viking rode the whale for a long time. Eventually, the sun sank below the horizon and night rushed in like water filling a sink.

The whale had been silent for much of the journey, but when the dark was truly upon them it sang again: *Sleep. It has been a long day.*

"I don't need sleep," said Trygve.

"Neither do I," Luna said, even though every bone in her body ached. "I'm riding a whale. I should be awake." Her nerves were frayed, and her eyelids were holding up a crate of bricks, but she would stay alert, stay conscious, stay curious, see what there was to see . . .

. . . a forest, endless and green. Caribou lumbered between trees; a lynx tracked a vole in the snow; a pine marten gripped a branch; a fox snuggled with her kits. The woods were not silent, but every sound Luna heard spoke to a deep, delicate, balance, as fragile as a quiet morning.

Then there was a *snap*, and a *riiip*. A hole opened—no, not opened—*tore* itself into being. The world shuddered. Out of the tear, corruption spread like fire on dry paper, until the whole forest was consumed by darkness and decay—not good, black soil, but a poisonous sludge. The animals grew sick and weak, and they died, all of them, except one: a bear, big and black-furred. It was searching for something, and it was desperate, but the search was fruitless. It rooted through fallen trees and mouldering leaves, unable to find whatever its heart so clearly longed for, and then it looked up to the sky, which had grown red as a bonfire. The bear moaned, softly, without hope. Luna thought it was the saddest sound she had ever heard . . .

Her eyelids lifted. Clouds. Endless clouds. She stared, silently, without thought, her mind as empty as the sky. Muscles began to awaken. Luna propped herself onto her elbows. Something grainy and itchy was beneath her arms. She was no longer on the ocean, but she could hear waves, beating against a shore.

She swivelled her head up and down. Above: indigo, edging the clouds. In front: the water, vast and grey as a thunderhead. Below: a pebbly beach, half rocks, half fine grit.

Then, far, far away, well past where the water rolled into breakers, a whale breached. It raised its tail and beckoned, once, twice, then goodbye, before slapping into the sea like a thunderclap. A wave like a wave.

She realized Trygve was standing near her. A strong wind blew, and his body shivered.

"What happened?" Luna asked. "How long was I asleep?"

The Viking shook his head. He looked as bewildered as she felt.

"If you slept . . . I think I did too. I do not know how. The whale spoke of sleeping, and it was dark, so I could not see much, and then—it was like I was a ghost again. A ghost before you . . . before the world broke. I was in one place, and then I was here. But between the two places, I recall nothing."

"Where *is* here?" Luna asked. It felt like they were back in Newfoundland, although this was a different part of the island.

They both looked around. If they had slept, it had been for a day, because night was spilling over grass ridges and snowy fields. In the distance they saw hills, dark and desolate, looming over an open grassland gone flat and rust brown. It was very quiet, but for the sound of the air whistling over the flats.

Then Trygve pointed. "I don't know where 'here' is, but I can see what *is* here."

"What?"

"Your father. And that which holds him."

Luna sucked in her breath. There, flickering in the hills, was a light faint as a morning star at the edge of a sunrise: a flash of blue and, around it, a waving, dark distortion.

Before Luna could speak, Trygve said, "Follow me," and began striding over the long, dead grass.

They moved in silence. The onset of dark did not clear out the clouds, which knotted around the moon. Every now and then a star peeped out to wink at the ground below. Luna felt a little jealous of Trygve's ability to walk without touching the ground, because the further they went, the wetter her toes got. The ground was springy and spongy. When her feet pressed into it, the land would sink and water, icy and dark, would soak her shoes. It was a little like walking through the sick smoke, except the wet here did not come from corrupted dirt. This water was cold, but it was natural to this place, and it was everywhere.

The night went from blue to purple to black, but Trygve radiated a faint light. Luna used his ghost glow like a torch. The land remained wet, but they were not in a swamp. A swamp is a flooded forest, and there were no trees here, just an undulating, mushy plain. In the brief moments when the clouds broke and moonlight washed the land, Luna could make out the edge of a marsh: slim reeds swaying by ponds and creeks. Beyond all this: the black hills, clad in a thin shell of snow.

Luna thought about what would happen when they finally found Gale Hair and Big Bear—thought on it until she carved a hole in her head that she retreated into.

In her mind, Luna sang a storm that wiped Gale Hair into tatters. Her father's essence would remain, though, unharmed. She wasn't sure how, but she would figure it out—how to harness the storm so it only harmed what she wanted. Then, Big Bear would come back into his body, and they would hit the road again—wandering and wondering and free of the dead, free of their fights, the world around her healed, her family—*her* world—healed . . .

The dead can't rest until the piece of the Heart is returned, came the voice, accusing and honest, in her head. *And you can't control the storm. You can only unleash it.*

Luna tried to shake off the thought, the nagging doubt, but it was stubborn, and it had claws. The conversation on the whale played in her mind, over and over.

If she wants to return death to its place, she must first return life to where she robbed it from. Where was that?

Whales only know so much about land sort of things. What is the purpose of a pinecone?

Luna remembered saying something about seeds, but then her attention shifted to her feet, which were thoroughly drenched. *Not much land sort of things around here*, she thought.

They had reached a place where the reeds grew thick. A stream, white and frothy, ran down from the hills in a cold rush and divided into countless channels. Luna wasn't exactly sure where they should be going, but she did know if she was to return the pinecone to where it came from, they had to find a forest.

But trees were a hundred miles away from this flat, wet plain.

"Watch where you step," Trygve said, as he moved through the tall grass. Luna followed behind, but for a moment she was distracted by a light that quickly flashed amidst the sedge and cattails. It looked like a piece of lost essence. She thought, *Dad* . . . and began to walk towards it, but Trygve saw her move and said, "Luna. With me, please." That whisper of a command, soft but stern, made Luna roll her eyes, but she obeyed.

Silence descended again, broken only by the sound of squishing feet and the tinkling rush of the stream. Luna struggled to keep up with Trygve, partly because he moved fast, partly because she kept seeing things—shapes, shadows, shades—and would stop to look at them. The curiosity in her heart was unquenchable, and it had grown in strength out here, in the dark, with nothing to see but vague outlines against an endless bog.

Luna was watching cattails clatter like wind chimes when a glowing ball, the size of a fist, floated over the grass. It resembled the ball that had emerged from her father, but somehow, it was less *alive*. It flickered from yellow to orange and back again, over and over; although, if she looked closely, there was an occasional flash of green. The ball hovered, then dipped, and hovered again before it bounced in the air. No noise came from it, but its movements spoke as loud as a child shouting, and what it said was, *Follow me.*

Luna smiled, and thought, OK. In the distance, Trygve walked on, moving without looking behind him.

The light bibbed and bobbed. It looked like it was dangling at the end of a fishing line. Luna could not tell if the glow was warm, but she thought it might be, and suddenly she realized how *badly* she wanted a warm place to dry her feet.

She followed the ball as it bounded over the ground, even though the mud was clingy, sucking, sticky . . . but that was OK. Because once Luna held the little ball of light, that tiny sun would warm her up and dry out the black water that crept up her legs . . .

"Luna, *stop!*"

She looked up. Trygve had finally turned, and now he was moving towards her, fast. Luna looked down. Water pooled around her knees. The light still hung in front of her. Again, she wanted to follow it, even into the waters that closed in all around her, waters now dotted with a dozen shadows, wispier than Trygve at his faintest, smoky creatures with outstretched arms and blank, fog-wreathed faces.

Luna stepped forward.

Trygve yelled again, and this time he pulled something out of his belt: his axe. The scout had looked insubstantial earlier that night, but now, with his hands comfortably wrapped around the wooden axe haft, he looked fierce and solid. Trygve lifted his arms and held the weapon high over his head.

That light drove the curiosity out of Luna's heart and replaced it with fear—and the realization that she had just walked into something she might not be able to walk out of. Her blood ran cold as the water creeping up her body. The blackwater had not overtaken her, but it was not far from doing so.

Trygve threw the axe. It sailed through the air in a perfect arc. Luna thought it strange that such an excellent throw would miss its target, which must have been the ball of light. But then she heard a thunk, and a scream, and saw *behind* the light.

A creature, squat and muddy, maybe half the height of an adult, but wide as a child lying on its side, hunched in the water. Trygve's axe was lodged in its shoulder. Its misshapen face had long tusks, its large hands ended in dirty talons, and its skin was mottled with brown and purple splotches. In its claws was a stick, and at the end of the stick was a string, although in the dark it looked more like a trail of clear snot. That sticky line was attached to the ball of light, but the glow was no longer yellow and warm. It had taken on the pale, white complexion of a dead fish.

The claws that held the stick that held the stickiness that held the light dropped everything to clutch the axe in its shoulder.

Luna named it: Fisher Demon.

"Ya yawny jinker! Puts a hurt on me, ya did," it howled, although it seemed angrier than injured.

The Fisher Demon gestured at the shadows behind it, and they moaned and moved, scratching the air around Luna. Their faces stretched with empty longing, and Luna knew: these were the shades of those people who had followed the light into the rushes and reeds and drowned. Their wet ghosts had come back to tempt the living to visit their muddy homes and stay as their guests, forever.

The Fisher Demon's voice gurgled like swamp water as it screamed at Trygve. "Sure now what was that for? I'm just fishing! The first child to cross me shaky-bog in a season, and ya throws your sharp stick to drive me off. Wants her all for yourself, does ya, ya chalk-skinned gom?" The Fisher Demon's muddy eyes rolled into the back of its head for a moment. They scanned the land in front of them with barely disguised greed and fixed on Luna.

Then the creature lunged at her.

She did not have time to think, so her mind became an animal's: all reflex and reaction. Luna grabbed the pinecone with both hands and held it over her head. Briefly, she recalled all the pain of the past few days—losing her father, fighting the Again Walkers, chasing Gale Hair.

Then Luna aimed all that pain down the gullet of the Fisher Demon. A storm is a song, and all the notes danced for her. A peal of thunder and a gust of wind swept over the low plains. And everywhere, the waters rose at Luna's command. The Fisher Demon had light at the end of his stick; she had a squall at the end of hers.

Luna exulted in her power.

But then she realized how much the water truly *was* rising. High, higher, the bog came: frigid slime, black as midnight, *schlucking* up Luna's waist and then chest.

The Fisher Demon was caught in the cold tide too. But despite the axe sticking out of its body, it was smiling: a piggish, greedy grin, the greasy smile of a gambler with a good hand who doesn't need to bluff.

"Made the waters rise, did ya? You're doing the work for me! I'm the bog's belly, ya dim nuzzle-tripe. Water grows me home. You're just giving me more to work with. Poor little lamb . . . ah well. I likes a lamb chop."

The Fisher Demon moved through the bog effortlessly as a fish, its limbs parting land and liquid, swimming through clotted mud and tall grass as easily as the boggy blackwater.

Luna breathed hard; her stomach had gone as cold as the water, but her mind was still sharp, all ferocity and fight. She shook the pinecone again; ice speckled her face as the wind flecked moisture in the air, but this just egged the Fisher Demon on. The ghosts that followed it knotted themselves into a sickly purple fog.

Now the monster's claws were close enough that Luna could see the mud caked on them, the strands of grass stuck between brown fangs in an open mouth that stank of bog gas and the drowned dead.

A rustle of movement, a great splash. Trygve was in front of Luna, standing—and she could see, he was *standing*, feet planted in the mud, firm and solid now—between her and the Fisher Demon.

The Viking grabbed his axe, which remained lodged in the creature's shoulder, wrenched it free, and brought it crashing down, over and over again. Still, the creature stood; its skin chipped away like it was made of wet wood, but the monster was not defeated.

Luna felt her face glow with anger, and she brandished the pinecone again.

Trygve turned around, his eyes desperate. "Stop, Luna! The water gives it power!" the Viking yelled.

He screamed and swung his axe again, and the weapon thudded once more into the Fisher Demon's sodden hide.

The monster only seemed mildly annoyed and gave the Viking an obscene grin. "Water don't just help *me*, chalky. There's more than me hunting ye two."

It gestured with one of its claws.

Luna turned to see what the Fisher Demon was pointing at. When she did, her guts sank to the bottom of her sopping feet.

There, striding across the dark grass, were shadows: misshapen, crooked, and bent, but large and powerful, with iron sinews and angry strides. There were five of them, all clutching spears and swords, and, though it was dark, Luna could see they held their weapons in lobster claws and tentacles, webbed hands, all gone pale from an unlife unlived in the deep. For these were the remaining *aptrganga*, the Again Walkers. And they walked, again.

13

Luna's mind melted from fight to fear as the *aptrganga* approached the Fisher Demon. The monsters looked at each other with something like wariness. Saltwater dripped from the coral-studded face of an Again Walker. The Fisher Demon's piggish eyes glinted. Then a grunt passed between them, and they all turned to advance on Luna and Trygve.

The Fisher Demon reached them first. It swung a taloned hand at the Viking, digging three scratches across his stomach; they were not deep, but they were a wound. The Viking grunted, then swung his axe again, but the thing only laughed.

Voices gurgled over the bog, words forming around tongues like sea slugs, tumbling over teeth of coral, arising from lungs that bellowed in and out like a pufferfish.

"Come back to us, Trygve. Join your warband again. Let us see with your scout's eyes—ours have grown too used to the abyss." One of the warriors winked with giant squid eyes, and his companions made a squelching noise like a boot caught in the mud. Luna realized they were laughing.

Trygve was holding his stomach, a grimace on his face. Faint lines of energy—*his essence*, Luna realized—bled from his wounds between his fingers. His other hand swung his axe in wide, sweeping arcs. It was enough to keep the Fisher Demon at arm's length, but the monster looked amused, and the spirits of its drowned victims were clamouring over themselves to snatch at the Viking.

The laughter of the monsters, the gusting wind, Trygve's screaming, her own heartbeat, all pounded in Luna's ears. She wanted to do anything, everything, and felt as if she was doing nothing.

Another noise broke through the din.

It was a gurgle, of sorts, but not the watery laughter of the Again Walkers. This was a *gluk*, followed by a saw-throated *kawaaaak aak,* then a deeper *hok hok*. It was the wind croak, and it came down from the sky followed by two ravens, calling, beckoning.

Luna felt an arm wrap around her chest. She began to scream—in terror, but also, from shock. The limb was cold, like it had been stored in a freezer. Then she looked up and saw Trygve's face.

"We have to *go*," he said.

The Viking pulled her tightly to his chest, his arm supporting her from underneath, and Luna gasped: it felt like she was pressing her body into a bed of snow. Trygve was moving as fast as he could, which was difficult in the bog; she felt each one of his giant sloshing steps as they retreated from the Fisher Demon and the Again Walkers. She could see over the Viking's shoulder, and what she saw shook her: all the creatures that hunted them were together, a sort of nightmare huddle of fangs and damp teeth and clammy scales.

"You still quick, Trygve," yelled an Again Walker with a head crowned by waving sea urchin spikes. "But we still catch you. You betray; we make you pay. Run, run: we find you, eventually."

"You'll find my axe!" Trygve screamed back.

The thing smiled and drew a barnacle-clad finger across its throat, while his companions whispered their queasy, bubbling laughs.

Trygve ran a few more yards until they were about the length of a city block from the Again Walkers. That was when Luna, shivering uncontrollably, with an effort that drained her remaining strength, reached up, pushed his arm away, and splashed into the water.

"What are you *doing*?" the scout hissed. "They will be on us at any moment!"

"I don't think so," Luna said. "Look, they've stopped." And indeed, they were not moving, neither Fisher Demon nor the Again Walkers. They massed, and mocked, and beckoned. But they were not advancing towards Luna and Trygve.

The ravens, in the meantime, croaked and cawed from the roof of a home that Luna was certain had not been there a minute ago.

It was the strangest house she had ever seen. It was made of the land itself, with grass for a roof, and empty windows cut into the dirt, and it sat on the bog, all alone and out of place, like a toy that had been dropped on the floor and never picked up. Without hesitating, Luna began to run towards it, but Trygve simply stood there, staring, his eyes wide and white.

"Now what are *you* doing?" Luna screamed.

Her feet *schlucked* over the mud as she ran up to Trygve. She had steeled herself for the cold touch of his skin as she grabbed his hand, but he had gone as soft as melting clay.

No time to think on that. She could still, for the moment, pull Trygve, and she yanked him into the hut. It was dark, and exceedingly cold, but at least it was dry on the inside. Otherwise, there was more dirt, an old firepit, wood stacked in a pile, and ash. Nothing else. No furniture or art or craft was there; everything about the hut suggested abandonment, emptiness, and loneliness.

Unbidden and unfed, the firepit roared to life. Luna and Trygve looked at each other in surprise over the flames.

Luna was anxious and sweating, but trying to take in her surroundings, to not let the danger nearby overwhelm her.

The Viking was very different.

"Trygve," Luna said. "You—you were solid back there. You had a body. You were dripping water—I can see it drying on the floor."

The Viking grunted. "I know. Or, truly, I don't know. I don't know why my body has returned."

"It hasn't. It's gone again."

Trygve looked down at his hands, saw through them, and screamed in frustration.

Luna wanted to calm him, but there were more pressing concerns. She walked to the open door of the hut and looked for the creatures that were hunting them.

It was still very dark, but she could see the Fisher Demon and the Again Walkers, shadows in the distance against the greater dark of the night. They were no longer jeering for blood. Instead, they milled around the bog, yelling, grunting, and grumbling. The ravens flew in loops around the hut. Occasionally, one of the Again Walkers would lurch towards the building, but whenever they did, a bird would swoop down, croaking its defiance, causing the shambling dead to retreat with a curse on their wrinkled lips.

"Thanks, birds," Luna whispered. Then the Fisher Demon screamed at her through the dark.

"Think you're safe, do ye? The black birds gave ye a little sanctuary. A little piece of the land, eh? A dry place on the peat." It spat: a long, thick gob of snot and saliva. "Maybe me and me mates could follow ye. We'd get pecked for our trouble if we did, which I don't fancy. But anyway, we don't have to. Because peat burns. And I like my meat well done."

It began digging with its hands, using its claws as shovels, and soon it was lumping mud and muck in a pile. "Only a little while 'fore I gets to the good stuff. Good black turf to make a fire that burns long and low. I'll smoke ye out, or I'll roast ye for Sunday dinner."

Worry began to gnaw at Luna. On one of Big Bear's assignments, she had learned about peat: clumps of long dead plants pressed into a dark mass that people used to fuel fires. Fear ran down her spine again like icy rain.

She stepped back inside the hut. She and Trygve were safe for the moment, but that moment did not seem like it would last very long.

But now a new problem presented itself: Trygve was sitting on the dirt floor, his expression stony as a mountainside, staring into the fire.

Without turning his head, he asked: "Why is this happening?"

"I'm not sure," Luna said, her brow creased. "The ravens are helping for now. But they can't stop a fire, and that's exactly what those things are trying to light. They're trying to burn us out. I can probably summon a storm to delay them, but that's only going to make the

Fisher Demon thing more powerful. I think it grows with the bog water."

"Not the cursed birds and monsters!" Trygve moaned. "Why—this?" He held up a translucent hand. "I woke up from a thousand-year sleep with no body. Then I had one again—arms and a chest and my good right arm. But I lost it again, and now I'm . . . *here*."

"Are you seriously only thinking about *yourself* right now?" Luna snapped, and the Viking hung his head. "If you're going to sit there feeling sorry for yourself, you can at least try and help me figure out how to fight what's out there, because what's out there is trying to *cook us alive*."

Trygve turned his head away. Luna wanted to scream in frustration. Instead, she took a moment to compose herself.

"Maybe you can figure out what this place is. It might give us an answer as to why you keep getting solid and disappearing and going solid again," she said, her voice growing just a little softer, but remaining firm.

She sat down on the other side of the fire and stared into Trygve's eyes.

"Think about when you've gotten your body back," she said. "Every time it's happened, you've been protecting someone. You said it yourself: the more purpose a spirit has, the more solid it becomes."

Trygve looked at her with cloudy eyes. "The ravens mentioned that. And more."

"What do you mean?"

The Viking stared deep into the flames. "They said, 'You need a true beginning to reach a true end.' I have been avoiding telling you an important part of my story since I met you, and I am sure that is why we are here. The whale, the ravens, say we need to know the past to fix the future. You paid that passage. I haven't." He looked up. His eyes were focused, although what they focused on seemed outside of the hut. "It's time to tell you how I died."

Luna watched him. On the one hand, she felt like, of all the times for telling a story, this was *decidedly* not the moment. On the other hand, she needed Trygve. He had helped her track Gale Hair. He had fought the *aptrganga* on the back of the whale. He had tried to warn her when she plunged into the Fisher Demon's bog, and when she ignored him, he had faced the creature in battle. For so long, Luna had longed for an adventure all her own, but without her companion, her *friend*, she would have died many times over. If he had a story to tell, she was obligated, many times over, to listen to it.

Besides: hearing Trygve's tale was not just a matter of doing right by a friend. It *had to be done*. When Luna told her story, she unlocked her truth, as well as the next step in their journey. It had hurt. Talking about how she had won—no, taken—the pinecone felt as thorny as a bramble bush. Her story contained a mistake, one Luna still had to fix. But in the telling, she had learned what was broken. If the ravens and the whale were right—and Luna believed they were—the world needed a true story before it could be healed. Trygve still needed to finish his.

She nodded at the Viking. "You're ready?"

"No," Trygve said. "But facing this shame is not a choice. I told you a story. But only part of it. And I think that's why I am fading away again. Only part of me is here. The rest is what I have yet to tell you." His eyes glowed, briefly, and Luna wondered if ghosts could cry.

The Viking's voice was soft. "You broke something. Snapped that seed cup. And it was hard for you to tell the story, but you did. You are braver than me. I do not mean that with resentment. You showed me the way." He swallowed.

"I . . . I broke something too."

The fire crackled, orange and red, the glow absorbed by Trygve's face. His expression was empty. Then he sighed and told his story.

14

Years and years and *years* past telling, I sailed with my lord as *húskarl*, and that means I was a warrior. My people—farmers and smiths and warriors alike—came here seeking a new home. We sailed from *Grœnland* and around the Sea of Worms, so named because the creatures that live in it devour the wood of boats.

"Our longships carried good stocks of wheat and water, but we knew we would have to find food where we landed, for we had never sailed so far from our home place. We were afraid—but proud! Because we were going to show the world a *new* world at the *edge* of the world. No challenge was too great for us, no water too wide. Can you understand such a dream, Luna?" the ghost asked.

She nodded, thinking of all the times she had tried to set off on her own.

"I scouted the first island we came to, all grey, hard and sharp, with no plants, just great rocks long enough so two men could lie on their backs, heel to heel," said Trygve. "We named that place Helluland, the Place of Flat Stones. There was nothing to eat there, except some white foxes."

"Go on," Luna said, remembering the dying fox in the sick smoke.

"Then we sailed to Markland, which means the Forest Place. The hunting there was good. But there was nothing but woods. Deer and bear and trees, forever. So, we sailed for many leagues, past shores filled with birds and beasts and so many fish they made the water boil with their swimming, until we landed at a new place. This place.

"The boats came ashore in the breaking surf, and it was I, Trygve, whose boots first touched the sand. It was I who scouted the hills and headlands, until I found the flowers and fruit that gave this country its name: Vinland. The Place of Wine. Green plants grew here, sprouting fruit we could eat, or make into drinks to make us forget how long we sailed. And my lord was proud of me. He gave me a gold armband."

Trygve showed Luna his arm. For the first time she noticed the ring-shaped outline there, set against skin as pale as the moon. Whatever treasure was there, whatever trinket Trygve was so proud of, had rotted away over the long years.

"What else did you find?" Luna asked.

Trygve gazed into the fire. "I found places to fish, and hunt, and I found beauty. Great, sweeping beauty to rend your heart, or fill the songs of a dozen skalds. And I found . . . people."

Luna held up her hand. "You told me no one was here when you arrived."

The Viking looked away. "I lied."

A scrabbling noise scratched the night air. It came from above, and both Luna and Trygve looked up at the ceiling. Then came the rustle of a deep, beating flap. Luna looked through the square hole cut in the side of the house. The two ravens pecked at a dead mouse laying in the wet dirt. Beyond, she heard the grunts and slobbering laughter of the Again Walkers, and the chuff, chuff, chuff of the Fisher Demon digging out chunks of peat.

Trygve sighed. "There *were* people here, already. We called them *skraelings*."

"Is that what they called themselves?"

"I don't know."

Luna shook her head. "Then how about we just call them . . . people?"

The Viking nodded. "Fine. There were people. They were hunters and fishers. At first, they kept their distance from us, watching us from the trees, or their villages on the coast. Some of us thought to trade with them, but . . . not the members of our warband."

"The ones who became Again Walkers?"

Trygve grunted. "Their fondest memories were of the old country, of raiding the coasts of Mercia and Anglia. They were hungry to fight the *skrae* . . . the people. So when we saw them, we attacked. And the fight was not terribly balanced, for our weapons were made of metal, and theirs, of stone. But the people knew the land and had more than a measure of courage. They shot us with arrows from their bark-skin boats, or from high up on the cliffs. They attacked us whenever we bent to scratch our legs, or so it seemed."

"Can you blame them?" Luna asked. "You were on their land. You even admit, you attacked them first."

"I . . . you are correct, girl. The people had their ways. We had ours. And our ways were bound in blood and iron. When they gave us combat, we felt we had to repay it tenfold . . . "

Luna frowned. Shadows from the fire flickered on, and *in*, Trygve. He took a long breath, before he went on.

"One day my lord asked, 'Trygve, scout out a new winter home for us in this place. Find a location where we can escape the frost and the *skraelings*' arrows.' I searched a long time, combed every cove and hollow. For a time, I think I wandered through your witch woods—a strange forest, under deep enchantment. When I emerged from those trees, I found members of my warband. And then I found . . . "

He stopped talking. At first, Luna thought he was overcome by memories of his past life. But Trygve was staring into the fire again, and the fire, Luna swore, stared back. Its flames grew from hot coals that became the pupils in Trygve's eyes. Smoke poured out and filled the hut, like a curtain had been drawn across the world.

Then the smoke melted away. Luna's eyes widened, because the walls of the dirt hut were replaced by tall trees, a rushing stream, and a deep blue sky. She was atop the edge of a hill overlooking a river, standing in the midst—and the mist—of a Newfoundland day. Near her were a dozen men, tall and fierce, eyes burning behind round helmets. All clutched axes, swords, and long spears. Each sported a thick beard and the scars of many battles, and the biggest were cloaked in bearskins that made them look more ferocious than they already were.

One warrior stepped forward and pointed down a hill with his sword. "There!" he cried. "Those are the *skraelings* the scout warned us of!" And Luna saw two things that made her stomach drop.

First were the people the warrior gestured at: men, women, and children at the shores of the riverbank, alongside baskets of berries and fish. Their hair was black, their skin smeared with a red-brown paste. Clearly, they were families. Children chased each other while their mothers laughed. One of the men picked up a girl and threw her in the air, over and over, the same way Big Bear tossed Luna when she was younger. The little girl shrieked in delight.

Then the people looked up and saw the pale warriors on the ridge. Fear coursed through the group of families like wildfire. Screams of happiness became wails of panic. Some of the children ran for their mothers, who held their little ones tight to their chests. Some of the women began to cry, and some looked furious, like they wanted to charge the armoured men with their bare hands.

The other thing that made Luna gasp was the scout leading the war party. His hair and beard were the yellow of a pale winter sun, his eyes as blue as a shallow sea. It was impossible not to recognize Trygve. He stood at the edge of the band of warriors, a hand on the top of his axe. His eyes, Luna noticed, were not angry. No—he looked scared, worried, and more than anything, sad. Indeed, the sadness in his eyes made Luna think of Trygve the ghost, except this Trygve stood with the light on his skin and the blood pumping in his veins.

The Viking who had pointed at the people threw a spear down the hill. He screamed "Odin!" and the warriors rushed down the slope.

Below them, the men of the people's gathering party shouted and fit arrows to their bows. Most of the remaining berry pickers fled down the riverbank and into the woods with their children, leaving upturned baskets behind. One woman, her face lined with age and resolve, set her jaw, and picked up a rock.

Arrows flew up the hill. One of Trygve's companions fell, clutching a shaft buried in his throat, but the other arrows thunked harmlessly into wooden shields.

Soon the Vikings were on the handful of the people who stayed behind, unarmoured or holding stone axes for their defence or, in the case of one woman, an actual stone.

Luna had to turn away. When she did, she saw one Viking running away from the battle, the blonde scout, turning his back on the slaughter, and escaping into the woods.

Clouds of dark woodsmoke rose from the ground and descended from the sky, shadowing the vision under a dark grey cloak that was broken by a single, crackling fire. Luna was back in the hut, and so was Trygve.

They stared into each other's eyes over the fire. Then Luna began to yell.

"You were strangers in their home! They held their ground even when they were outnumbered, so their children could escape. They fought back even when they only had a *stone*."

Trygve's face was striped with smears of light; he was, indeed, crying. "I know that was hard for you to see, girl. Just know that it was . . . immeasurably hard for me to live through it again. Up to that moment, I had told myself I was brave. That my friends were brave. But in truth, we were as cruel as frost giants. Before that day I had only led men to water and berry bushes, or herds of deer for hunting. Never to an 'enemy.' I knew we raided towns and villages, but I had never *known* . . . no, I never *admitted* what that meant. That there were people in those places. Not just people . . . children."

Whenever Luna felt really angry, it was like a rubber band was tightening around her throat. Seeing the misery on Trygve's face, hearing the guilt in his voice, she felt that tension release, a little. But a thought occurred to her, and the tightness returned.

"You could have told me this from the beginning. Why did you lie to me?"

Trygve's face twisted; he looked like he had been socked in the gut. "I was ashamed! And I thought, by not telling you what happened, I could *avoid* a lie. Instead, my past would be . . . a story. I needed you to believe in me."

Luna was about to challenge him, but then she paused, and thought, and spoke.

"I . . . get that. I couldn't bring myself to talk about what happened by the Heart of the Forest until a whale and some ravens basically told me off. We all tell stories, or keep stories to ourselves, to get by," she said, remembering the fight with her dad over the meaning of 'home can be anywhere.' Big Bear had been trying to protect her with a story. Now she wanted to hear the rest of Trygve's, so she could rescue and hold her father and be home, anywhere, again.

"So what happened after you ran into the woods?" Luna asked.

The Viking looked into the centre of the fire. "I stayed in there, away from everyone. I had a skin of wine, and I finished it amidst the trees, thinking I could drown the memory of what I had seen."

"Did that work?"

"For a little, as happens with wine. Then I grew lonely. Fearful. But if wine makes one forget their memories, it also robs your legs of their skill. I slipped down some rocks and hurt my ankle so badly I could not walk—that part of my story, at least, was true. It took me a long time to find the strength to move. When I returned to our camp some days later, my people had already gone to their ships, to find a new place to spend the winter. I suppose they thought I had been killed by those we attacked, seeking their vengeance. I am sure they did not mourn me, because I had been a coward. I found one of our huts. An empty, abandoned hut. And I went inside, and it was cold. And I lied down, and I slept. Alone."

Sadness twisted Luna's heart, but it was mixed with something like understanding, because for the first time, she felt as if things made sense: why they were here, in this home, and why he had been so hesitant to enter it in the first place.

"It was *here*," she said. "This is where you died."

Although she knew that if *this* was the hut, it likely had not stood at this exact spot, and would not have lasted so long without crumbling to dust. The ravens, she suspected, called this hut from the memory of the land.

Trygve nodded. "And now, it seems, I may die here again. At the hands of those I betrayed."

Luna said "*No*," with so much conviction Trygve jumped. "No," she said again, softly. "You will *not* die here again. And you did *not* betray them. You ran away from doing something terrible. You keep telling me coming back as a ghost is bad, but you know what's worse? Coming back as a *monster*. Like those things outside. You might be dead, but you're still human, and that's because running away from your companions kept you human."

She noticed something: shadows. Of course, there had been shadows in the hut before. But these shadows were cast by the firelight hitting Trygve. The firelight hit Trygve—but did not pass through him.

Luna stood up, walked over to the scout, and laid her hand on his shoulder. It rested there, and in the fire's glow, his body was not cold to the touch.

"I could have stopped them," Trygve said, shaking his head.

"You could have tried, but there were a dozen of them, and one of you," Luna said. "They would have killed you. But yes, they *need* to be stopped, now. They're still a curse on this land. They're evil, and right now they're standing between us and my dad. You can do this. You're stronger now, and you have me."

She squeezed his arm.

"You wanted a purpose," said Luna. "I think it's more than just helping me. Together, we're going to make sure those Again Walkers don't ever walk again."

15

Trygve stood up, pulled his axe from the loop on his belt, and swung it in an arc through the firepit. The flames licked the axe-head, but they did not go out. It was as if the weapon had found its own new purpose: as a torch.

The Viking looked at his flaming axe and smiled.

"What just happened?" Luna asked.

"I am learning it is best not to question these things," Trygve said. "I awoke after death. I travelled the whale roads—*on a whale*. I became mist and a man and mist again. And I met a girl, a storm singer who speaks with the voice of Thor. I would not have believed these things when I drew breath. Now that I do not, I can accept them."

"Thanks, Trygve," Luna said. "Although my storm singing isn't helping much right now. All that wind and water made things worse."

Trygve frowned, walked over to her, and this time, *he* put his hand on *her* shoulder. It wasn't cold, but Luna couldn't help backing away a little, as the axe in his other hand was on fire.

"A storm can be many things. My father was a farmer who never picked up a sword, yet he loved Thor above all other gods. He swore the best time for sowing was after a thunderstrike. Storms brought destruction, but also cleansing rain. He always said, 'After Thor visits, you can plant anything. Just put seeds in the dirt and watch them grow.' You have fought great enemies Luna, but, like a storm, you have also helped things grow. Me, at the very least."

He grinned, and Luna returned the smile. But fear still soured her stomach. She knew there was no time to celebrate. Not yet. Because the Fisher Demon and the Again Walkers were still outside, and beyond them, Luna's father remained a captive of Gale Hair.

But first, they had to deal with the monsters on their doorstep.

Luna led the way outside. Her hand dug into the pouch of her hoodie, where she ran her thumb over the pinecone. The two ravens took off from the roof of the dirt hut, soaring into the air before her, wind croaking, like heralds announcing her arrival.

Trygve followed, flaming axe in hand. Then the Viking stopped and stood, quietly, in the night chill.

"I had never been solid when I was not fighting. And when I fought, I had no time to savour the feeling. I had forgotten what it felt like to feel the wind on my skin," he said. "My real, solid skin—not the essence that lays beneath it."

"How does it make you feel?" asked Luna.

"Finer than if I had eaten the most decadent feast. And now I will expose that skin to the claws of a demon, and the weapons of my old warband."

"And how does *that* make you feel?"

Trygve thought. "Like boarding a boat to cross the ocean. Exciting and terrifying in the same breath." His eyes took on a measure of determination. "I welcome the terror. I will face what is in front of me, even if it destroys me. Better to take fate into my hands than die hiding in a hut."

In front of them, the Fisher Demon stretched, and the Again Walkers chuckled.

"Ye've come out to die, then?" said the Fisher Demon. "Very accommodating of ye. And I see ye've brought fire? Well, ye needn't have. We brought our own."

It stepped aside, revealing a pile of peat, heaped into a small mound. The Fisher Demon took his stick with the dangling light and touched the glow to the turf. In seconds, a fire erupted, building itself into a blood red blaze.

The Fisher Demon had lit the fire, but he kept his distance from it. The Again Walkers did not. One of them kicked the mound, sending a flaming clump of peat sailing towards Luna and Trygve. Where the burning turf landed, the fire spread; they may have been in a bog, but this fire burned wherever it found grass, and there was grass all around.

Trygve charged, a war cry on his lips. Two of the Again Walkers laughed and ran at him. One swung a heavy stick, studded with coral studs, at his legs, while the other brought a wicked sword in an arc towards his neck.

Trygve ducked the second blow, but the first one caught him in the thigh. He leaned over like he was in unbearable pain, and Luna screamed as the creature with the coral club smiled and pressed its advantage. But just as it was upon him, Trygve jumped backwards to dodge its swing, causing the Again Walker to lurch forward, unbalanced—which was when the flaming axe crashed into its back.

It grunted and fell into the mud, but it was not dead; Luna heard it curse and try to pick itself back up. In the meantime, its companion was forcing Trygve back on his heels with a series of quick sword jabs.

Luna swung the pinecone at it. A tight coil of wind lanced out from her arm, striking the Again Walker in the stomach and knocking him to his knees. Trygve advanced to finish it off, but then the laughter of the Fisher Demon rang out over everything.

"Nothin' spreads a good fire like a bit of wind, am I right, fellas?" it cackled.

And now Luna saw: the wind she had called had pushed the fire around the battlefield, and in moments, the entirety of her vision was cloaked in heat. Red and orange flames crackled on tussocks of grass, and they seemed to *hunger*, to expand, not randomly, but in the direction of everything that was fighting on the bog.

One flame leapt out towards Trygve, who was busy trying to force the Again Walker with the coral club back into the mud. The fire singed both of them; the Again Walker howled and rolled in the grass, causing the blaze to spread farther, while Trygve used his cloak to beat out the flames licking at his right leg.

Luna cursed and swung the cone above her. A spiralling column of rain formed over her head, extending into the sky, and when she dropped her arms a cloud of water surged forward, dousing the fire on Trygve . . . but also on the Again Walkers.

One of the creatures chuckled as it brushed dead, wet embers off its spines and spikes and fins. Some of the other monsters were knocked over by the squall, but they seemed content to lie in the muck for a moment, *slurping* their limbs through the mire. But the Fisher Demon simply stood with an enormous smile stretching its face, revelling in the moisture that speckled his fangs and arms, the bog water growing around its ankles, all the accumulated wet sinking into its skin.

"Thanks for that, girl. I loves the damp. Makes me fat. And happy. And *strong*."

It bent its short, powerful legs, and leapt: over the Again Walkers, over the smoking remnants of the grass fires, and onto Trygve. Two taloned feet planted in the Viking's chest, forcing him flat onto his back in the mud. Trygve still held his flaming axe in his right hand and brought it up in a sideways arc that caught the Fisher Demon on the side, but the monster was too strong to be deterred. Instead, it slashed down with one of its hands and gouged Trygve's chest.

The Viking screamed.

The Again Walkers laughed.

The Fisher Demon said, "Time to finish ya off, fool."

"No," Luna cried, and her voice was amplified into the ripping *crraaAAAaaack* of a thunderbolt that passed over the monsters in a shockwave. The force of her cry threw the Fisher Demon back on its sharp heels for a moment and forced the Again Walkers to reach out their arms and claws and tentacles to steady themselves. The creatures, drenched in hate and saltwater, picked themselves up and stared at Luna across the bog, the peal of her thunder cry still crackling in the air. Deep in the cold eyes of the *aptrganga*, she saw something like a measure of respect take hold.

Then Luna's thunder brought rain. The Fisher Demon giggled. The Viking moaned. And Luna stood there with the piece of the Heart of the Forest in her hand.

She felt helpless—she had power, but it kept working against her. Her storms were useless; they only gave the Fisher Demon strength.

Luna took a breath and cleared her mind, and as she took the air in, clarity came too.

This power is working against me. I'm feeding what is trying to kill us. She looked at the pinecone in her hand. *But seeds aren't supposed to make storms. They make . . . life. Lots of life. Life like I saw in the forest: trees bound together by their roots.*

She remembered her dad, smiling with his eyes at her in the rear-view mirror, squeezing her hand.

Like a family.

The memory drove out her helplessness. Then the voice in her head was replaced by the voice of her friend, a Viking who was helping Luna find her father and had just told her a story about his own: *After Thor visits, you can plant anything. Just put seeds in the dirt and watch them grow.*

You can plant anything.

Luna looked at the pinecone—the seed cup—in her hand. *I hope so*, she thought.

She felt the dirt beneath her feet. It was soft and yielding, and it was calling to her. She held the broken piece of the Heart of the Forest up, whispered a silent prayer, and plunged it, deep down, into the earth.

The cone sank into the soil. Immediately, glowing green lines of energy coiled up from the mud and braided over the bog, an explosion of bright emerald threads rushing to infinity. The green became vines and the vines spread like a sunrise.

Luna saw time stop and speed up all at once. She saw soil and moss. The pinecone was now a tree, surrounded by other trees, their bark silver or black, their leaves broad or needles.

Trunks continued to erupt from the ground like the teeth of a vengeful dragon. Each one spiked an Again Walker, thrusting through their bodies in one clean motion. The monsters did not bleed, but they howled in shock. But not for long.

As the trees grew into the monsters, they grew around them too: scaly bark lapped onto sea-sodden skin and over it until the Again Walkers had no mouths left to howl with, or eyes to see with. Each individual monster, a nightmare of mutation and corrupted nature, was transformed, in the space of a minute, into a tree. In less time than it took to tie a shoe, the host of *aptrganga* had been replaced with a calm, quiet grove of twisted, but healthy, balsam fir.

Three pines grew into the Fisher Demon as well, their branches and trunks throwing its arms to the side and forcing its face to look at the sky. The demon was pushing back against the greenery, and he was strong; by sheer will he kept the wood from spreading over his skin, and for a moment, it seemed as if he would be able to force the trees that grew into him back into the earth.

But then the land seemed to sigh, and pulse, and the trees shot to their full height.

The demon was thrust several feet into the sky, his feet dangling off the ground, his arms enveloped in leaves and branches, only his face poking out to curse at the world.

The monster wheezed and snorted and breathed in a wet, heavy panic. All around it, as far as the eye could see, the forest grew in a dark green explosion. Birds flapped onto branches, branches interlaced over hollows, and the night sky was driven away in a rush of air that smelled of dirt and dead leaves. Already, the sun was shining, as if it had never dropped below the horizon, and purple clouds were tearing themselves apart to reveal a deep blue sky.

Trygve pulled himself to his feet. He walked to the Fisher Demon, trapped in a tree, unable to move its head and tongue.

"Damn . . . ye," it managed to gasp at the Viking.

"Damned me," said Trygve. "But no longer."

Luna saw the axe in his hand; it was soaking wet. The fire that had burned there before was quenched. She thought the scout might finish the Fisher Demon with his weapon, but instead, Trygve dropped the axe back into his belt. Then he held out a hand and shut the monster's eyes as it moaned in protest, as bark crept over its ears, its cheeks, and its mouth, finally leaving a squat, misshapen, white birch standing in the middle of mounds of red and purple lichen.

The ghosts that had followed the Fisher Demon did not seem to have much will or direction, other than a need to drown anyone who walked into the bogs. Now, the new forest—*was it new,* Luna thought, *or had it always been here?*—was swallowing them.

Before the battle, the shades had formed a rolling mass, a cloud made of shadows. Now this cloud was melting, growing wispy and faint. A wind blew over the forest, and what was left of the ghost-cloud flew into the spaces between the fast-growing leaves, where it faded and vanished.

Other ghosts were streaming into the forest, drawn to the trees: hundreds, *thousands* of spirits. Most were nothing more than a faint discolouration in the air. Some had manifested into fully formed, if transparent, people. At first, Luna recoiled, scared by this onrush of the dead. But as she watched, she felt an air of calm, and contentment, and *stillness* settle on the land, and her heart.

Some of the ghosts seemed nervous, but most wore expressions of eager anticipation. They flitted in between rows of branches and fat leaves, or black trunks and pine needles, before they wobbled, wavered, and finally sizzled into nothing. Luna did not think the ghosts suffered. Indeed, they seemed to rush headlong into the new growth, and the faces of the more formed beings even betrayed the slightest smile before they faded into nothing, or maybe, Luna thought, everything.

Finally, the spirits were gone. Only branches, and leaves, swayed in a slight wind. Luna stared at the trees, at the restored forest, for a long breath. Then she whispered, "That . . . that was something."

"How did you know?!" Trygve sputtered. "How could you tell the cone would just—grow?! And at that pace?"

"I didn't know," Luna said. "But after you told me that story about your father, I figured maybe I didn't need to know. I just needed to plant something after a storm." She grinned, but only briefly. "Don't get me wrong, I'm very happy about this—but why are you still here, Trygve? I think I just regrew the border between life and death, right? Isn't that why all the ghosts are disappearing?"

"I had assumed so."

"So why didn't you?" asked Luna. "And where is Gale Hair? And my dad?"

"Always questioning," Trygve said, but he was smiling ear to ear, and his face remained whole. "We have work to do, and it needs to be done quickly, before I too fade into the forest. I will remain by your side until I have fulfilled the rest of my purpose, which is to protect you, and help you find your father. As for where he and the thing that took him may be . . . I have a feeling we will be able to answer that question shortly. You regrew the forest and, by doing that, laid the path to where we must finish this."

Trygve was looking to the north. The trees had grown so far and fast they covered the world in every direction—except that one. There was some forest there, but it quickly thinned out into a place where the land was open and unshaded and the blue sky had turned cold grey.

Here, among the trees, Luna and Trygve's faces were brushed by a passing breeze; while there, under the clouds, the grass was flattened below a wild wind: fierce, unrelenting.

A gale.

16

Trygve dropped the axe to his side, where it hovered, trembling. This comforted Luna for two reasons: because the Viking had a weapon and was ready to use it; and no less importantly, because he was as scared as she was.

"That's where we need to go," she said. "The forest is everywhere but there. Something is stopping it from growing, and I think we both know what—or who—that is."

"What about your seed cup?" Trygve asked. "Shouldn't we dig it back up? We will need it for this next battle."

"I'm not sure where it's gone," Luna said. "And I'm not sure I need it anymore."

"Your powers of perception are remarkable," the Viking said, "so I am a little surprised you have forgotten that little piece of a tree has the power of a god. Let me refresh your memory: it saved us on the back of the whale, and it slew an army of Again Walkers and a bog demon. We are about to face, as you once said, a ghost other ghosts were scared of. She has a power beyond any I can summon. I contend that I would not mind having such a weapon by our side for the upcoming battle."

"Yeah, but that battle will be against a thing that got loose *because I snapped the pinecone from the tree*," Luna said. "If it's planted now, I don't think it's a good idea to un-plant it." She said these last words with a heavy, 'don't-argue-with-me' finality—and realized it was the same tone her father used with her when he didn't want to debate.

That way of speaking clearly had an effect on Trygve, who nodded and said, "My trust in you outweighs my need for tree magic."

"Let's go," she said, but the Viking held a hand up.

"Please," he said.

He looked to the horizon and began to sing, softly. It was a low, slow, mournful tune. It made Luna think of snow kissing the ocean, or rain on green leaves, or a high cliff carved by the wind.

The lonely music briefly pushed away Luna's urgent need to set off. For just a moment, she let the world go still as she listened.

The Viking finished, and sighed. "That was my death song," he said. "A custom of my people, sung before battle. A chant to remind me of who I am, and a plea to the gods to let me feast at their table when I am gone."

"But aren't you already dead?"

Trygve looked straight ahead. "I have not ruled out the possibility that I can become *more* dead."

Luna felt anxious, but the presence of her friend made her legs feel a little less wobbly. This was the time for settling things, come what may.

She walked, steady and surefooted, through the forest, slipping between trees as they grew thinner and sparser, to the place where the grass was blown flat by the wind and the woods were a memory. Soon, she was in a moor, at the bottom of a long, spongy field of lichen peppered with pink sheep laurel and sea thrift. In front of her, the land rolled into a gentle hill, above which soared the long, cloudy sky, a place of vast openness and boundless air.

Luna looked at Trygve. A silent acknowledgement passed between them: they were near the end of the quest.

"Onwards and upwards," Luna said, and they went up the hill.

The sky was knit like a grey blanket. As they walked, dark clouds sent out slashing lines of cold rain. The water ran down Luna's face in thin trickles. When she first arrived in Newfoundland, almost two weeks ago, the feeling of ice water kissing her face would have bothered her. Now, after so many adventures, Luna was almost comforted by the rain.

It was not long before she and Trygve were surrounded by houses and gardens. They could hear waves battering a shore, and over the hills, the dark sky descended onto a darker ocean, dusted with narrow whitecaps. These were not the dirt huts Trygve's people built, but cottages like Gordon's: squarish, built of wood, with neat rows of windows and steep sloped roofs topped by chimneys. But also different from Gordon's home, because Gordon's community was full of people, and life, and this place was abandoned. No laundry lines decked with drying shirts blew in the breeze. No smoke puffed from the chimneys. No chatter came from radios or televisions or humans. No cars sat in driveways, because what had been driveways were now discoloured grass. All was quiet, but for the wind, and the pattering hiss of the rain.

They were in less a village than the sad memory of a village. The yards were overgrown with weeds. The windows were cracked. The drapes were torn and stained. Luna watched curtains blow in, and out, in, and out. *Like they are breathing*, she thought. Rotting rope, rusted lobster traps, and fishing floats—drained of colour from disuse and neglect—dotted the wiry grass. The empty second stories of the homes were angry eyes, watching her and Trygve.

Yet if the houses felt alive, nothing else did. This was a forlorn place. Luna remembered Gordon telling stories about communities that lost their people but kept their memories.

She made a kenning: *the hollow place.*

They walked to the top of the hill. There was a house here, all peeling paint and rotted wood. The yard was thorns and ivy, rocks and turf, which spread in a green carpet over . . . a roof? Yes, a roof made of grass, jutting from the hillside, and beneath that, a door that led into the earth. But it wasn't a house. Once more, Luna remembered Gordon's stories. *Cellars. Like a fridge made from nature. A place to put things.*

But she also sensed that 'things' were already there, in the dark, under the earth. A hungry, tense energy infused whatever was behind the door. There had been places Luna had explored with Big Bear where they both felt a prickle on the back of their necks. 'Soft places,' her dad called them, where it felt like the spirits pushed against a barrier between life and death. This place, Luna thought, had the consistency of melted butter, and it called to her.

"Whatever is in there does not want to be disturbed," Trygve said.

"I know," said Luna. "But 'in there' is where I need to go."

The scout grunted. "Then I will follow you."

Then the croak wind split the air. The ravens flapped down onto the eaves of one of the ruined houses, swivelled their midnight heads, and *quorked.*

Luna nodded at them. "I planted the Heart. But I still need my dad."

The ravens cocked their heads. One raven clawed at the ground, leaving faint scratches in the dirt. The other snapped its beak open and shut, two dark knives slashing the air, *clickclackclick*.

Luna knew the ravens would not follow her underground. Birds were creatures of the sky. But she appreciated their presence, here, under the open sky at least.

"Thanks. For your help back on the bog," she said.

Quork, said the ravens. They were perched above the shattered remains of a window. There was just enough dirty glass left in the frame for Luna to make out a splotched, dim reflection. She saw: an eleven-year-old girl in a hoodie, tights, and sneakers. Her clothes were muddy. Her head was crowned with curly auburn hair that was beginning to twist into knots from a lack of washing. She was slender, but not thin; her shoulders were round, and her arms were strong. There was dirt on her face, which had the flushed pink of her mother mixed with the woodsy, dark complexion of her father. Her eyes were green flecked with gold: grass in the sun.

The girl looked very familiar, and much older than Luna remembered.

She turned away from the window and walked to the door that led into the earth. She pushed it, and immediately, her face was awash with the smell of air that hadn't been breathed for a long time: stale, empty, bone dry.

Luna stepped inside the cellar followed closely by Trygve, leaving the door open behind her. The space was not big, but it was cold; goosebumps quickly prickled on her arms. *It really is like a fridge*, she thought. And not just because the air was chilly, but because food had clearly been stored here. There were still sacks, empty and ragged, arrayed against rows of sagging shelves. The walls and floor were dirt; she could see roots and stones running through both thanks to the weak sunlight that streamed in behind her. All around were cans and hooks the colour of dried blood.

Suddenly, she felt an urge, overwhelming, as strong as the suck of the tide, to *leave*. *Leave leave leave* went a voice in her head, hammering against her brain like breakers on a rocky beach. She loved her father, but he would understand, she had to run, she had to go, because to stay here was death and worse than death: emptiness, a dry afterlife of bitter solitude, forever.

Luna turned back towards the door to the outside world—*the hollow place*—and stopped.

The door was blocked.

Gale Hair was tall. She had strong shoulders and an angry face. Her eyes looked sunken, as hollow as the empty homes that lay behind her. Her dress was in tatters. Black hair blew behind her, fierce and free, although no air had moved in that cellar in a lifetime or more. Her eyes were narrow and dark, her expression pinched and suspicious, and the air around her seemed *infected* with anger and despair and fear.

The spirit moved towards them. She floated above the ground, even though she looked as solid as any living thing. Then her mouth curled into an expression of scorn, and she spoke: "Little lady. Little *thief*. Have you snuck into my cellar to steal from me? Show some manners and curtsy to your elder."

It struck Luna that if Gale Hair's words were angry, and the air around her was poison, her voice was surprisingly pleasant. Her accent was laced with the same sort of sing-song melody that Gordon spoke with. But there was something about her voice that made Luna want to obey it, even though she was the kind of kid who pushed back on her dad's commands and couldn't remember the last time she'd curtsied for someone.

"What . . . " Luna stammered, "What would I steal from you? Your cellar is empty."

Gale Hair's eyes narrowed. "You little fool. My cellar grows fatter and fuller with each passing day. You should see what has just arrived! I took some of it a little while ago, but now I have come into possession of the whole thing."

The spirit gestured to a far corner of the room.

Luna looked, and when she did, her heart lifted even as her stomach sank.

Big Bear lay in the dirt, curled up like a sleeping child. His skin was pale, and pulsed with a dim, blue glow.

Luna ran to him, but Gale Hair screeched, "*Stop*."

"I will not," Luna said.

The spirit sneered, and there was venom in its voice. "Stop, thief, or I will crush what essence he has left."

Luna snarled and stopped, for the sake of her father, but her rage was like the wind off an iceberg.

She turned on Gale Hair. "Did you call me a *thief*?" Luna said, her eyes narrowed. "How dare you—you—you *thing*! Give me my dad back!"

She looked to her father again. His eyes were closed, but something white and bright sparkled on his eyelashes and beard—frost. The ice crusted and sparkled, then spread, slowly, but inexorably, all over her father's body, just as bark had overwhelmed the Again Walkers and the Fisher Demon thanks to the Heart of the Forest . . .

. . . which was growing behind one of the *shelves*?

Luna tried to keep a poker face, but she almost screamed. Seeing the tree was almost more of a shock than seeing her father. A quick second look confirmed it: a small, young tree, a sapling, really, was growing out of the cellar dirt. A pinecone hung off one slender branch, white, flecked with bits of green. This was, unmistakably, the cone she had used to summon storms and fight off monsters on land and sea. That pinecone could only grow off one tree . . .

Luna's eyes caught Trygve's, who glanced towards the Heart and gave her the quickest, faintest nod; he had seen it too.

Gale Hair looked at Luna with contempt, then at Big Bear with something like... protectiveness? As if, despite her earlier threat, he was a toy that she treasured above all her possessions—not that there were any in this empty, dusty cellar. But the spirit did not look anywhere near where the Heart grew, and Luna knew: *She has no idea that it's there.*

This gave her some hope, but that little light was in danger of being smothered by the darkness that steamed off the monster that had captured her father.

"That 'whole thing' is my father!" Luna yelled. She had come too far, through too much, to see her dad stolen away at the last moment.

"What are you on about, child?" the spirit sneered. "You think my prize belongs to you? That man is my own, to do with what I please, how I please, as I please." Her voice was cold and cruel, and when she finished speaking, a fresh, thick crust of ice crackled onto Big Bear's eyes and lips.

Luna wanted to scream, but wrestled control of herself, and simply cried out, brief and desperate. The spirit smiled and began to—there was no other word for it—sing. A high, tinkling note filled the cellar, and the louder it grew, the more snow and ice caked onto Big Bear's beard.

Desperately, Luna tried to calm herself. *Gale Hair is consumed by anger. If I make her angrier, she might hurt dad more,* she thought, which was the moment Trygve raised his axe, let loose a war cry, and charged.

Luna—who had heard the Viking's true story, seen him shudder in front of the Again Walkers, watched him weep for his past sins—was a little frightened by the reckless courage stamped on her friend's face. Gale Hair, on the other hand, sized the warrior up with casual disdain. As his axe came down, she raised her hands, and the weapon stopped. Then she gestured, faintly, lightly, and the axe-head flew back.

As it did, the spirit let loose a high, keening cry. It was the same sound she had unleashed on the ocean, but louder, more concentrated, like noise had spun itself into pain. The scream unravelled every nerve ending in Luna's brain before it set them on fire. She felt nausea jump from her toes into her throat. Retching, she sank to the floor, snot running from her nose, tears streaming out of her eyes.

But Trygve was even worse off. He had entered the cellar solid, but Gale Hair's scream had ripped him raw. The hands that held the axe faded into thin smoke. The weapon clattered to the ground, while Trygve screamed in agony. But as loud as his scream was, it was a whisper compared to the wail that continued to shake the room.

Finally, Gale Hair's screech stopped, though echoes of her voice still dripped from the walls, like blood oozing from a fresh cut.

"I'm sorry, Trygve," Luna managed to gasp through her tears, still unable to stand.

"Don't be," the ghost scout whispered, wincing as pieces of himself fell to the floor and disintegrated. "A warrior who will not die to save his friends is a poor warrior indeed."

He picked himself up to attack again.

Luna smelled the dirt beneath her, the cold, strong musk of the earth. Trygve's words echoed in her mind: *A warrior who doesn't die to save his friends is a poor warrior indeed*. She grunted, then pushed herself up by her elbows and knees until she too was standing—between two ghosts.

She had wounded the Heart of the Forest. She had endangered her father, and now she was saving him. She had brought Trygve here, and she would bear the brunt of the next scream.

17

Luna stared into the face of the thing that she was sure would kill her: red-rimmed eyes, streaming black hair, a pale mouth with long jaws that opened wider than any human mouth could stretch. She looked into that maw and down its red, cavernous throat, and it was as if she saw the scream form before she heard it in her ears; although, in truth, the sound slammed into her chest first. If a shout could become a winter blizzard and a sledgehammer all at once, this one did just that.

Luna collapsed on the ground, lights exploding in front of her eyes, blood running down her nose.

Then, with an effort that scraped out the last shreds of her soul, she stood up again.

The spirit sucked in its breath once more, but as it did, Luna began to speak, quickly, gasping, "You know that's my father. You say you want to do with him as you *please*? That's . . . evil. He's my *dad*. I don't *want* him. I *need* him."

Gale Hair's mouth shrank to a normal size, but her hair remained wild and unfettered, and her voice still echoed with the power of a winter storm.

"Liar! Everyone knows I keep the best stores in the finest cellar in town. Why else would you be here, but to take what is mine, from my tins to my man?" the spirit said. It didn't scream that time, but Luna still felt her knees turn to water.

"I am telling the truth," Luna said. "And here's another one: I don't *care* about your food or your supplies. I haven't come to steal anything, and I don't think anyone else is either, because this village is empty. There's no one here. Except my dad—*he* is the only reason I am here, and he is coming home with me."

"She speaks truth," said Trygve, who was still fading in and out of existence. His voice had gone as dry as the dust that coated the shelves of the cellar. "Whatever you once protected is destroyed. Whatever you once watched over is long gone. And that man belongs to his daughter."

The spirit sneered. "Gone? Where did my people go? This is our home, as it was for our parents and their parents before. Why would we leave the soil of our blood?"

As scared as Luna was, she invented a kenning just then: *blood soil*. The words, she immediately knew, were terribly powerful. They tied the land and the people who lived on it in a knot, so tight and tangled she couldn't tell where one ended and the other began. Every kenning was like a story; this story told of people who would shed blood for the soil and guard the soil with their blood.

Except there was no living blood left to fight over this soil.

"Open your eyes. Your people *did* go. Look outside," Luna said, pointing to the open door, and what lay beyond: the houses, their rotting walls, and the yards choked by weeds.

Gale Hair turned around. Her eyes widened, and for a moment Luna thought she had seen the truth of the situation. But then the spirit made a moaning sound. Fear and fury knotted together into one anguished note, then unleashed itself in another scream.

This time the yell was not directed towards Luna or Trygve, but rather, at the entire world. It was as if the hollow place had finally found a voice after so much silence, one that carried every pain and injury that happened there, with no room for love, laughter, or peace.

As the scream echoed, the walls of the cellar shook, shimmered, then began to fade. Luna looked around and saw that she was now outside of the cellar, but still in the hollow place—except it was no longer hollow. They were in the past, but not the past of Viking times. This was a not-so-long-ago. There were cars parked in front of some of the houses; Luna guessed they had been popular around the time when her grandparents were her age. Woodsmoke rose from every chimney. Tables were laid outside the houses, and on each one fish were split open, covered in salt. Clothes dried on laundry lines and children ran underneath them, shrieking with laughter.

But the children were the only ones who looked happy. The adults—two groups of them—were gathered in front of a house, and they all looked grim. Some wore coveralls and rubber boots. The others wore dress shirts buttoned up to their necks and ugly neckties. Both groups were angrily gesturing at each other, and the tension between them hung thick in the air. A woman in a simple dress seemed particularly worked up. Her face was red, and her eyes flashed with contempt for the people she was speaking with.

"Where would you and your clipboard and that stupid tie put me and mine?" she asked one of the official looking men. "Ship us to St. John's so I can work as a secretary? These hands are for salting fish and keeping my yard free of nettles, not typing," she huffed, holding out her storm-callused palms. "Not that your hands have ever seen a day's honest work."

"Take it easy, Mrs. O'Riordan," said one of the necktie men. He was speaking in what he clearly thought was a calm, reasonable voice. What Luna could see, as plain as day, was that the more he tried to soothe the woman, the angrier she got. Luna couldn't blame her. The man had an expression on his face he probably wasn't even aware of, the barest trace of a smirk that said, "Calm down and listen to me, because I know better than you."

"You won't need to go as far as St. John's," necktie man said. "You and yours will just be a little ways aways: to Twillingate, or down to Summerford, and you can salt fish all you like. But you'll have *roads*. And *schools*. And a doctor to fix the kids up when they're ill."

A man in coveralls spattered with salt shifted his weight and said, slowly, gently, "Maybe's not so bad, Angie. Maybe there's something to their plan. Maybe we can—" and he stopped, and fell quiet. Because he may not have had a smirk on his face, but he was still telling Angie O'Riordan to calm down, and this only stoked her fire.

She turned on the coveralled man with derision in her eyes and a scream on her lips. *I know that scream*, Luna thought.

"And maybe I married a coward!" Angie snapped. "How can you listen to this nonsense? How can you put any trust in these weasels? These crows, come to take our lives and pick over the bones?" Tears began to glisten in her eyes; in a fury, she wiped them away. "For God's sake, our parents and their parents and *their* parents gave us this." She gestured at her house, and the land and water that surrounded it. "Not to throw away when something better came along, but to *protect*."

"Angie," said her husband, the man in coveralls. "There's a life outside of here. And everyone else knows it."

"He's right," said necktie man, smooth, smirking. "We've been talking to the others in the community, and they're leaning towards resettlement. It won't be so bad. You'll have a new house, with new appliances. New furniture to show off to all your girlfriends . . . "

"Enough of both of you!" Angie yelled, and she turned away and walked towards a cellar. She spoke loudly, without turning around, "I swore to guard this, and I won't be bought off like a banker." She said 'banker' like it was a particularly offensive curse word. "I'm off to put my stores in order. You wants to give me a new house, but this is my *home*. It'll be a cold day in hell before I leave. But sure, to hear you all blathering on is close enough to the fact."

Luna followed Angie—Gale Hair—into the cellar. Once she crossed the door, the air shimmered, and they were back inside the cellar of now: an old, empty hole, dug into the side of the hollow place. Dust was settling on the floor, shaken from the rafters and the walls by Gale Hair's screams. Big Bear still lay curled in one of the corners, while Trygve was barely keeping his essence together.

And somewhere in that room, Luna knew, the Heart of the Forest grew, green and alive.

There was Angie, floating amid the shelves and cobwebs. She looked at Luna with eyes that bored into the soul, and she spoke: "This is my cellar, that I dug. There is my home," she said, pointing outside, "where I split and salted fish. This, little girl, is my home, and none leave it, least of all myself."

At first, Luna thought of telling Angie to take a deep breath, to put things in perspective. That was the advice Big Bear gave Luna whenever she was upset. Then she thought of the people who she'd just seen try to soothe Angie with peaceful voices. That approach hadn't worked when she was alive, and whatever anger Angie felt had grown stronger in death.

If Angie did not want fake courtesy—if she wanted honest anger—Luna decided she would get it.

"*Listen*," Luna said. "I know you want it to not be so, but look with your eyes, and not just your heart. Everyone is gone. And you should be too! Nothing is keeping you here. A house with no people in it is just a house. A cellar with no family to feed is just a hole in the ground. Actually, you know what? I don't care if you go or not. Stay, for all I care. *But give me back my dad.*"

Angie looked at Luna for a long moment. Then she said, with no power behind her voice but the simplicity of the answer: "No."

"*No?!*"

"No. You're right girl. Fine. I admit it. The land is empty, my people are gone, the cellar is ash. It doesn't matter. It's still where I'm from, where I belong. Even if it's made of loss. Now, who else here knows that feeling? Of what it's like, when your heart's made of sadness same as a home is made of timber?" She pointed at Big Bear.

"That's not true," Luna growled.

"You say you speak the truth, but you avoid this one, though it's right in front of your eyes. I saw it, the night I met you. Oh, I remember. Coming out of the woods and seeing your dad, and knowing, then and there: here's a man with grief on his brow. Here's a man with fear in his soul, as afraid of losing his heart," Angie pointed at Luna, "as I was angry at losing my home. So now I'm giving him a chance to leave all that misery behind! I'll freeze him here, and neither of us will have to lose anything, or anyone. Ever again. He won't have you, but that's all right: we'll be homes for each other, forever."

Angie's wild eyes narrowed. "And there isn't a damned thing you can do to stop it, for having some company as sad as myself is my greatest desire, and I'll shout the world to pieces to bend it to my will."

Now Angie smiled, grimly, but her voice was tainted with bitterness.

Luna felt sick. She knew there was a pit in her father. A hole in the whole. The death of her mom made loss take up so much space in his head and his heart, which was why he was always worried about losing Luna.

Except, Luna thought, *was he?* He took her around the world while he searched for good stories. That life let Luna *learn*, and stories—from the myths that fed her appetite for adventure to the truths she had shared with Trygve—were her teacher. *Stories make stories*, she thought. Her story of Big Bear being worried all the time was the first chapter in another story she had told herself for the past year: of a girl who wanted a quest and was willing to be a hellraiser to go on one. Angie was telling a story too: of a woman who screamed for what had been taken from her, who wanted to keep Luna's father—another soul cut by loss—by her side, forever. It didn't matter that Angie didn't know her dad, or even cared about him (because if she did, why would she take him from his daughter, the person he loved the most?). Angie saw someone plagued by darkness, and the story she told herself was that her long nights would become brighter with company.

A part of Luna felt sad for Angie. But it was a drop next to the ocean of how much she needed her dad.

My father is not darkness, Luna thought. *He's a light for me. I'm a light for him.*

Heedless of the ghost's earlier warning, Luna walked to Big Bear. Angie began to open her mouth to scream again, but Trygve's voice piped up from the floor, high and hollow, tired but still strong: "She has searched for him across village, sea, bog, moor, and magic forest. Give her a moment. You, of all shades, understand how loss can devour a heart."

Luna gave Trygve a grateful glance. Then she watched, fascinated, as the hair that streamed so wild behind Angie's back stopped whipping in the air. Just for a moment, it grew still. The spirit looked at the Viking, and—so faint it could have been missed in an eyeblink—nodded.

18

Most days, Luna woke up before her dad. When she was younger, and the absence of her mom felt deeper, she would spend those quiet, grey mornings snuggling into his arms, as she often snuck into his room in the middle of the night. That habit stopped when she got older. These days, she was even starting to sleep in past him, a role reversal neither father nor daughter had truly been prepared for.

Still, more often than not, she was the first one up. Her routine on those mornings was to walk into Big Bear's room with a book and, with her head on his chest and her feet propped up on the wall, start reading. He was a heavy snorer—once, a guest in a next-door room in a hotel had complained about the noise. Luna usually found the low rumble . . . well, not enjoyable. It was annoying, actually. No reasonable human being could put up with it unless they really loved the snorer.

And Luna did. She didn't *like* her dad's snoring, but it was comforting; it was normal; it was expected.

It was home.

"I'm sorry, Dad," Luna said. She placed her hand on his face, and even though his skin was freezing, worse than Trygve's, worse than the cold of the ocean or the icy mud of the bog, she kept it there.

And in that moment, when it was just the two of them, as it had so often been on those quiet mornings, Big Bear stirred. His face, ever so slightly, twitched. Luna thought it might have been the air from outside blowing on his beard, but no: her father had moved. A fraction of a fraction of an inch, but he had moved.

Luna's mouth fell open. The movement was too small for Trygve to have seen, but she turned to him and, with a look, tried to tell him something important was happening. Trygve held her stare for a few seconds, then nodded, just barely, and looked toward where the Heart of the Forest grew through the soil of the cellar.

Luna did as well. She did not know what exact power she could summon from the Heart, but she knew this: Angie was strong. While she lived, people had tried to force her off the land. But connection to the soil was a part of her soul. That link sustained her life after death.

That link fed the bond that made her the match of an army of Again Walkers.

But though Angie was linked to the land, the Heart embodied it: the life of the forest, the power of the storm. Luna knew if she held the pinecone, that force would be hers to command.

She looked back at her father for a long moment. Then she walked to the Heart of the Forest and placed her hand on it.

The air shivered. A roll of thunder made a low whisper in the sky, while a smell—green and dark and alive—drifted through the cellar door. Luna's eyes closed, and she breathed long and slow, suffused with the power of the cone.

But this time, she did not break it from the branch.

"Angie," Luna said. "Come here. I have something for you."

The spirit's fiery eyes widened, but she drifted over—probably, Luna thought, because she knew she could scream everyone in the room into a puddle of quivering nerves if need be. As the ghost moved towards her, Luna glanced at the tree: a little over half her height, slender but strong, rooted in the dirt cellar floor.

Luna had come to understand something about the Heart of the Forest. She had outwitted and defeated Billy, who had tried to feed on its power. For a time, she'd been able to tap into that power—at least, the kind linked to storm and wind. Later, she had helped an entire forest grow from this one pinecone. And now, in the cellar, Luna sensed a deep need within the tree and the tangled webs of life it was connected to. It was not something new; no, it had always been there: but she hadn't noticed it, maybe because she had been too concerned with her own needs, both the selfish ones (finding a quest) and the not-so-selfish (finding her dad).

Now that need was obvious, in front of her—and then, so was Angie.

Quick as a bird, Luna placed her hand on the ghost, while the other gripped the Heart.

A tight, sucking sensation—a *whush* of air and movement—and Luna saw what Angie saw, and what they both saw was everything: in the woods, and beyond. There were the trees, stretching to the mountains, and the ghosts moving between them, at peace and at rest. They heard the bird song in the leaves and the whale song on the waves and the moose song in the pines. They smelled the wind blowing over fields of trembling aspen and partridgeberry bogs, tasted salt in the air and snow falling on the bays. Luna took Angie's gnarled, clawed hand and put it on the tree.

"They took the land from you," the girl said. "That wasn't fair. It was cruel, made worse because it pretended to be kindness. But it happened. Now *this* is happening." Luna could see Angie wanted to struggle, but somehow, her love of her father, coupled with the Heart of the Forest, kept the ghost in check.

"I saw you when you were alive," Luna went on. "You have a powerful voice now, but you had one then, too. You used it to swear to protect your home, to guard it. Well, here is your chance." She moved Angie's hand from the tree to the pinecone. "This cone is part of the tree. The Heart of the Forest. And the Heart is connected to . . . I think, *everything*. At least, on this island. Everything you just saw, with me. So . . . *there*." She squeezed Angie's hand and the pinecone at the same time. *Cupping the seed cup.* "There is your home. Not just that house outside, or this cellar, but everything they are built on. Because home can be anywhere. Home is what you make it, and I think, truly, that you already made this island, all of it, your home."

Then Luna's eyes narrowed, and her voice took on its own cold determination, echoing the steely anger of Angie in the past.

"But *he* is my home," Luna said, gesturing to Big Bear, "and I am taking. Him. Back."

Angie's fire eyes blazed. She looked confused, annoyed, but also, deep past the other emotions: intrigued.

"And . . . if I say no?" the ghost asked, and Luna noticed how meek that terrible voice was when it wrapped itself around a question.

Luna was not feeling meek. She closed her eyes and felt the scales of the pinecone press into her palm. A wind shuddered the shelves. Moss erupted from the dirt. Roots snaked out of the cellar walls.

"Then I will not let go of this Heart. I won't hurt it again, either," Luna said. "I did that before, and it did no good. But I'll turn all of us in this cellar into the land and the trees. I did it to some monsters before, and I can do it again. And if I do, then you'll get your wish, and all of us—you, me, the Viking, my dad—will be parts of this home. Forever. You won't crave company anymore. You know why? Because you and I will be branches and leaves."

A vine snaked up the branch around Luna's hand. A hiss of heated ozone and static danced on her eyelashes. Angie's fiery eyes looked into Luna's green ones, but Luna stared back, thunder behind her gaze.

"Girl," the spirit said. "This community... the house, this cellar. It was my life. I lived and not-lived to save it. How are you different from the men who tried to force me off this land? You are offering me a home, but it's a forest, not this house, this cellar, *this* home."

Luna shook her head, and spoke, carefully but forcefully. "*This* home is ruins. You wanted to protect it and you couldn't. But *this* tree, the Heart of the Forest—it needs a protector, too. I think that's why it appeared in your cellar." Luna said these next words carefully. "Your old home is gone, Angie. I am so sorry for that loss. But the land your home stood on is connected to the Heart, and the Heart chose you to be its guardian. And isn't *that* what you've always wanted? To protect a place?"

Angie's eyes grew warmer . . . then dimmed, to the colour of a fireplace settling in for a long night.

"So . . . I'd stay here. I'd sort of stay . . . *everywhere*. That'd give me the last laugh on those twits in their ties" she said, and chuckled. "Plus, I did always like playing in the woods when I was a girl."

Luna smiled too, her first smile since she had dreamt on the back of the whale. "You can play, and watch over anyone who walks by the trees, and the trees themselves," she said. "You'll be *home*."

"*Home* . . . " the ghost whispered, like she was eating the word, feeling how it sat in her stomach.

And even as Angie said this, she began glowing. The shelves of the cabin seemed to smush together into a solid mass and stretch into trees, even as the walls of the building fell over, revealing dirt and bright white sunlight descending from a sky gone as blue as the ocean. The former shelves, now trees, spread their branches into arcs and fans. Ferns and brush burst out of the bottom of the cellar, until the dirt floor was a forest floor. The village itself—the *hollow place*—was now full of life and greenery, pine branches and dark ponds. The homes shrank away, to be replaced with moss, stone, and birdsong.

Angie stood amidst all of this, truly smiling, even laughing. And as she laughed, her 'ha ha ha' became a 'caw caw caw.' Her long black hair split into two masses and became feathers. Her head elongated and darkened, and where there had been a gaunt face with fiery eyes, now there was a black bill and a raven's curiosity and—well, the eyes remained the same. Hard and hot, observant and self-assured.

The Angie-raven flew high onto a branch, a branch attached to the Heart, the sapling now grown into a full-sized tree. A sound of fluttering, a rush of wind, and then the new, fire-eyed raven was joined by two other black birds, ravens that looked very familiar to Luna.

So there they were: the triple protectors of the Heart of the Forest.

Luna closed her eyes, smiled, and let her hand drop from the tree. All the connected images she had just held in her mind's eye faded.

Trygve was shaking his head. He was still not solid, but neither did he look as if he were about to be blown apart in a stiff breeze. Indeed, just then, a slight wind raced through the forest, and it passed through the Viking like long forgotten breath.

"Your bravery shines in a dark place again," he said.

Luna nodded and looked at the Heart of the Forest. Then she looked back at the ravens.

"You've been with me a long time," she said. "You're the only creatures on this island that explore as much as I do. You want to see everything, just like me."

Trygve nodded. "To see a thing is a raven's purpose."

The ravens, all three of them, stared down at the Viking and the girl, then looked at each other. And while birds can't *really* speak, these birds were not-saying, very loudly, *We saw everything. Did you?*

Luna nodded. "I saw enough. Now, just one more thing."

She walked around the tree, and there, lying amidst tea blossoms and twin flowers, was Big Bear. His eyes were still closed, but his complexion had returned, as brown as the bark of the trees that surrounded him.

Then he snored.

Luna laughed. Then she cried, and then she was doing both and holding her father's face to hers. He did not wake up, but he was still snoring. For now, that was enough.

Trygve whispered, "It is time, Luna. You gave Angie a home. Now you need to go back to yours."

Luna turned. Trygve stood there, but barely. He had almost completely faded away, although what was left looked content.

The Viking grinned. "You helped me find my purpose. But I am not going back to an un-life of haunting eaves and quiet places. You said home can be anywhere. So I am coming into my real reward. Angie will protect the land. I will *join* it. For me, home will be *everywhere*."

Luna smiled. "Thanks, scout. You proved your name," she said.

Now all that was left of Trygve was the faintest outline of a hand. Luna reached for it, and while she could not touch him, their fingers did briefly lace together, hers literally flowing into his.

There was a gentle *whuff*, a sweet summer breeze, and for a moment Luna was with her friend: a wind blowing across the long field that stretched down from the hollow place, then through a forest, across a bay peppered with icebergs, over ocean-carved cliffs and salt-washed rocks, into tinkling marshes and stony headlands.

Then it was dark. But not because she could not see; rather, it was nighttime.

Luna was in Gordon's yard. It was cold, and wet. A light was on upstairs. And beneath her, her father was propping himself up on his elbows.

19

Luna swept her arms around her father and cried, silently, into his shoulders.

She felt his hands come up slowly around her as he sat up, and knew he was confused, disoriented. But then he shuddered, and his tears splashed on her cheek.

Luna's emotions filled her throat, and she snorted.

"Ew," said Big Bear. "You snotted on me."

They both laughed—long and hard, a laugh that went back to crying, then switched to laughing again. A shadow appeared in the upstairs window: Gordon, checking on his guests.

Her dad stopped laughing, although he did not stop crying. Then he looked into his daughter's eyes and asked, "Luna. What just happened?"

Luna sat down in front of Big Bear. Storyteller that she was, she realized she had no idea how to start: with sleeping on a whale or hearing a Viking's story or summoning a storm or almost getting eaten by a bog monster or breaking the teeth of a forest demon or turning a ghost with a voice like terror into a raven?

Instead, she said, "I got lost again. I think you did too. But we found each other."

He smiled. "Yeah, we did."

She smiled too. Then she shook her head. "No, sorry, Dad, I take that back. *I* found *you*. It's a long story. You might not believe all of it. But I did. *I* found *you*."

He raised an eyebrow, and for a moment, she was worried: were they going to fight? Especially after everything that had happened.

But then he nodded. "OK. I . . . don't remember much. But I believe you." Another tear trickled down his face. "I know I'm tough on you. You're all I have. But I don't have you, do I? You're you. I'm . . . trying to remember that, even while I'm trying to keep you safe."

He held his daughter at arm's length. She matched his gaze, then decided she didn't want to be at arm's length anymore. Instead, Luna hugged her dad tight, and whispered, "I am me. And I'm yours too. We're what the other one's got. Always, OK?"

Then the big feelings came on them both and they just sat there, hugging, exhausted.

...

The days passed, long and blue and lovely. Big Bear and Luna still had a week left to explore the island, and they made the most of it: hiking, and climbing, and fishing with Gordon; Luna even caught a cod. Big Bear, on the other hand, caught kelp.

One evening, father and daughter walked into Gordon's kitchen and saw the old man grinning. When they asked what was happening, he hugged them both.

"My daughter is coming to visit. With her family!"

A few days later a woman named Liz, with carrot orange hair, grey eyes, and a fast smile, came to the house with her husband and son, a seven-year-old boy wearing an Edmonton Elks T-shirt.

The boy ran up to Gordon, yelled "Granpop," and threw his arms around him.

Luna and her father and Gordon's family all ate dinner together that night. Big Bear asked Liz about her work, and Gordon's daughter went on a long spiel about hard days, but good money. Then she looked out the kitchen window, at the streets and the harbour of Dove Cove, where the seagulls circled and the boats clinked against each other, as the sun sank into the sea.

"I miss this, though. All of it. The boy needs to know what the ocean smells like," Liz said.

"It feels like home, doesn't it?" Luna asked. She noticed her dad's attention quickly snap up.

Liz sighed. "It really does. No matter how long I'm away, how foreign this place can start to feel when I've been gone for too long, it's always home when I'm back. Speaking of: where do you call home?"

Luna caught Big Bear's eyes. He said nothing, didn't even change the expression on his face. Instead, he gave the smallest nod, gentle as a summer breeze, one that said without saying, *Go ahead.*

"Dad and me kind of make 'home' wherever we go," said Luna. "So I've always had a hard time thinking one place can be home."

"I can see that," said Liz. "My best friend I grew up with here went into the air force. I think her kids feel the same way."

"Totally," Luna said. "But after being here for a while—well, I can see how one place ends up being *the* place for you." Her thoughts travelled back to a dirt-floored cellar, and wild black hair stretching into raven wings. "I think now I get why you would want to stay in that place. And fight for it." In another corner of the room, Gordon was telling his grandson a story about getting lost in the woods.

After dessert, Luna walked into Gordon's backyard. The wind kissed her face, then slathered it with salt off the ocean. She breathed deeply, tasted spruce and ice and fish and dirt.

Gordon's home glowed in the oncoming night.

The place Luna thought of as home did too—the place she saw now, as she looked west, where the sun touched the sea and the clouds reflected all the collected light.

Then, as she turned back towards Gordon's, Big Bear stepped outside and waved to her. She waved back. They would set out again, soon.

Adam Karlin was born in Washington, DC, and raised in rural Southern Maryland. As a journalist he has written on war, politics, crime, archaeology, history, and the environment, but fantasy is his first literary love, and *Luna and the Heart of the Forest* is his first novel. In his spare time, Adam balances a love of being outdoors with intense indoor jags of reading, tabletop RPGs, and video games, but he likes to enjoy all of the above with his wife, daughter, and son.